DEMOCRATIZE WORK

DEMOCRATIZE

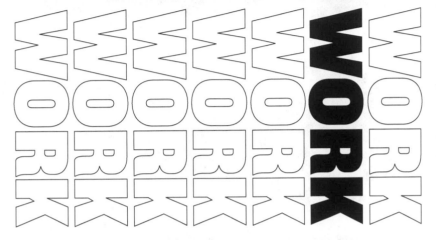

THE CASE FOR REORGANIZING THE ECONOMY

ISABELLE FERRERAS,
JULIE BATTILANA, AND
DOMINIQUE MÉDA

Translated by Miranda Richmond Mouillot

The University of Chicago Press
Chicago and London

The University of Chicago Press, Chicago 60637
The University of Chicago Press, Ltd., London
© 2022 by The University of Chicago
All rights reserved. No part of this book may be used or reproduced in any
manner whatsoever without written permission, except in the case of brief
quotations in critical articles and reviews. For more information, contact the
University of Chicago Press, 1427 E. 60th St., Chicago, IL 60637.
Published 2022
Printed in the United States of America

31 30 29 28 27 26 25 24 23 22   1 2 3 4 5

ISBN-13: 978-0-226-81962-4 (paper)
ISBN-13: 978-0-226-81963-1 (e-book)
DOI: https://doi.org/10.7208/chicago/9780226819631.001.0001

Originally published in French as *Le Manifeste Travail. Démocratiser.
Démarchandiser. Dépolluer*
© Éditions du Seuil, 2020

Library of Congress Cataloging-in-Publication Data

Names: Ferreras, Isabelle, editor. | Battilana, Julie, editor. |
    Méda, Dominique, editor. | Richmond Mouillot, Miranda, translator.
Title: Democratize work : the case for reorganizing the economy /
    [edited by] Isabelle Ferreras, Julie Battilana, and Dominique Méda ;
    translated by Miranda Richmond Mouillot.
Other titles: Manifeste travail. English.
Description: Chicago ; London : The University of Chicago Press, 2022. |
    Includes bibliographical references and index.
Identifiers: LCCN 2021054528 | ISBN 9780226819624 (paperback) |
    ISBN 9780226819631 (ebook)
Subjects: LCSH: Industrial relations. | Democratization. | Organizational justice. |
    Capitalism.
Classification: LCC HD6971 .M327513 2022 | DDC 331—dc23/eng/20220103
LC record available at https://lccn.loc.gov/2021054528

♾ This paper meets the requirements of ANSI/NISO Z39.48-1992
(Permanence of Paper).

CONTENTS

INTRODUCTION

For a Fairer, More Democratic, Greener Society

JULIE BATTILANA

When Sandra arrived in Boston from her hometown of Vitória, Brazil, everything felt foreign. Looking back now on those first few months, she shudders. Through another Brazilian immigrant, she had obtained housecleaning work shortly after settling in. She worked constantly, trudging home most nights after dark, too late—and often too tired—to spend meaningful time with her son. The work was arduous, the pay minimal, and the days long. She could not help but think the American Dream, or even just the chance to live a dignified life, was out of reach no matter how early she left for work or how late she stayed. Because she had been in charge of workers' safety at a factory before moving to the United States, Sandra also knew how toxic many of the cleaning products she was using were to her health and to the environment. So, when she heard about Vida Verde, a worker cooperative organized by Brazilian women immigrants, which sells housecleaning services using natural products that are healthier for domestic workers and for the environment, she jumped at the opportunity to join them—even though she did not know what to expect.

Joining has made a significant difference in Sandra's life. Not only have the other worker-owners been a source of information, support, and strength, but working on her own terms has also been transformative. "I feel like I have a superpower," she told me. "I am my own boss. I make my own schedule. I can't express how important this is. I now have time to take care of my son, and he is the reason I immigrated in the first place! I've traded in exploitation for autonomy."

By coming together, these domestic workers have built an organization that gives them control over their working lives. In doing so, they shifted the balance of power in their favor by becoming the worker-owners of a cooperative that offers a valuable resource to its socially and environmentally conscious clients: access to ethical housecleaning services that are worker centered and environmentally friendly. By letting them decide when they will work, how they will be compensated, and even how to adjust safely to a global pandemic, this power has changed their lives. In March 2020, when the COVID-19 pandemic sent Boston into lockdown, existing clients cancelled and new clients stopped calling; Sandra's and Vida Verde's work came to a standstill. Together, they decided to use some of the cooperative's funds to compensate each of the workers for lost business, giving Sandra some income during the three harshest months of the lockdown.

The level of control Sandra and her coworkers have over their working conditions may sound like a reasonable baseline for all workers. Indeed, access to dignified work, democratized governance, and a job that cares for people's and the planet's health is what every worker should have. Yet, this is not the norm for most people, especially in the informal and domestic economy. Workplaces remain largely hierarchical, most of them more authoritarian than democratic. As the philosopher Elizabeth Anderson provocatively puts it, "Bosses are dictators, and workers are their subjects."[1] Few workers have Sandra's power to influence the strategic decisions that affect their working lives. Such lack of control is associated with job dissatisfaction, greater mental strain, and damaged physical health.[2] Workers often have no say in pay equity (no wonder CEOs are paid 351

1. Elizabeth Anderson, "How Bosses Are (Literally) Like Dictators," *Vox*, July 17, 2017, https://www.vox.com/the-big-idea/2017/7/17/15973478/bosses-dictators -workplace-rights-free-markets-unions; see also Elizabeth Anderson, *Private Government: How Employers Rule Our Lives and Why We Don't Talk about It* (Princeton, NJ: Princeton University Press, 2017).

2. Robert A. Karasek, "Job Demands, Job Decision Latitude, and Mental Strain: Implications for Job Redesign," *Administrative Science Quarterly* 24, no. 2 (1979): 285–308; Jeffery Pfeffer, *Dying for a Paycheck: How Modern Management Harms Employee*

times more than the average worker in US companies[3]), in executive hiring, or in their organization's adjustments to health or financial crises. Instead, especially in nonunionized workplaces, control over these decisions is concentrated in the hands of top executives and board members who represent the interests of shareholders. Since power derives from control over access to valued resources, this disparity in control over strategic decisions results in a great power imbalance among workers, top executives, and capital investors, placing workers in a heavily disadvantaged position.[4]

Vast Power Differentials

This power imbalance is not new. Far from it. But for a time during the past century, the power pendulum in the United States swung slightly in favor of workers. For instance, the 1935 National Labor Relations Act (also known as the Wagner Act) established collective bargaining rights, opening the way for workers to legally strike, form a union, and jointly negotiate with executive leadership. But the Wagner Act did not (and still does not) protect workers like Sandra: agricultural workers and domestic workers were excluded, further marginalizing Black workers and other workers of color, who are disproportionately represented in these professions.[5] Nevertheless,

---

Health and Company Performance—and What We Can Do about It (New York: Harper Business, 2019).

3. Lawence Mishel and Jori Kandra, "CEO Pay Has Skyrocketed 1,322% since 1978," *Economic Policy Institute*, August 18, 2020. Accessed on January 18, 2022, https://www.epi.org/publication/ceo-pay-in-2020/. For longer-term executive compensation trends, see also Carola Frydman and Raven E. Saks, "Executive Compensation: A New View from a Long-Term Perspective, 1936–2005," *Review of Financial Studies* 23, no. 5 (2010): 2099–2138.

4. Julie Battilana and Tiziana Casciaro, *Power, for All: How It Really Works and Why It's Everyone's Business* (New York: Simon and Schuster, 2021).

5. Juan F. Perea, "The Echoes of Slavery: Recognizing the Racist Origins of the Agricultural and Domestic Worker Exclusion from the National Labor Relations Act," *Ohio State Law Journal* 72, no. 1 (2011): 95–136. Over 57 percent of domestic workers are Black, Hispanic, or AAPI while these workers make up 36 percent of the rest of the workforce. See Economic Policy Institute (EPI) analysis of Current Population Survey basic monthly microdata, EPI Current Population Survey Extracts, Version 1.0.2 (2020), https://www.epi.org/publication/domestic-workers-chartbook-a-compre hensive-look-at-the-demographics-wages-benefits-and-poverty-rates-of-the-profes sionals-who-care-for-our-family-members-and-clean-our-homes/; 57 percent of farm laborers, graders, and sorters in 2019 were of Mexican origin. See USDA, Economic

despite these restrictions, between 1910 and 1970, worker organizing, redistributive public policies, and investment in social welfare contributed to an increase in overall income equality, including a decrease in the income gap between Black and white Americans.[6] The 1970s and 1980s marked another turning point, however, as an aggressive neoliberal economic agenda—of which the economist Milton Friedman was one of the most vocal promoters—became dominant, stripping power from workers. This neoliberal form of capitalism has promoted the deregulation of markets, an exclusive focus on profit and shareholder value maximization, and domination by capital.[7] It has generated, and helped justify, massive levels of inequality. By 2014, the share of the country's total wealth held by the top 1 percent had surged back up from 22 percent to nearly 40 percent.[8] Forty years ago, 20 percent of Americans were unionized (a low number compared with other industrialized democracies); by 2020, a meager 10.8 percent of US workers were unionized.[9] During approximately the same period, CEO pay increased by 1,322 percent, while worker pay grew only 18 percent.[10] For most Americans, the promise of the American Dream—the opportunity to achieve upward socioeconomic mobility—has disappeared.[11]

The consequences of this concentration of power in the hands of a wealthy minority driven solely by profit maximization affect all of us. It has commodified workers, transforming them from human beings into mere "human resources" in service of profit generation. Markets, including the so-called labor market, decide who can work and under what conditions. Yet, markets are neither neutral nor fair.

Research Service analysis of data from US Department of Commerce, Bureau of the Census, American Community Survey (2018). Accessed September 2021, https://www.ers.usda.gov/topics/farm-economy/farm-labor/#demographic.

6. Robert Putnam and Shaylyn R. Garrett, *The Upswing: How America Came Together a Century Ago and How We Can Do It Again* (New York: Simon and Schuster, 2020).

7. For a deep dive into neoliberalism as an economic and moral doctrine, see Wendy Brown, *In the Ruins of Neoliberalism: The Rise of Antidemocratic Politics in the West* (New York: Columbia University Press, 2019).

8. Putnam and Garrett, *The Upswing*.

9. US Bureau of Labor Statistics, *Union Members—2020*, USDL-21-0081 (January 2021). Accessed September 2021, https://www.bls.gov/news.release/pdf/union2.pdf.

10. Mishel and Kandra, "CEO Pay Has Skyrocketed."

11. Bhashkar Mazumder, "Intergenerational Mobility in the United States: What We Have Learned from the PSID," *Annals of the American Academy of Political and Social Science* 680, no. 1 (2018): 213–234.

They are characterized by biases and imperfections that favor some of us and disadvantage others.[12] Women and racialized groups were barred from accessing the labor market for much of history, and their contributions are still disproportionately undervalued today in the form of unequal compensation for equal work. The market can be understood as a series of negotiations between actors with unequal power. As those with more power prioritize their financial returns, they perpetuate inequality.

Those at the bottom of the power hierarchy are not the only people harmed by this situation. It is detrimental for all of us because it threatens the institution that protects our rights and freedoms: democracy. "As for riches, let no citizen be wealthy enough to buy another, and none poor enough to be forced to sell themselves,"[13] Jean-Jacques Rousseau presciently warned in *The Social Contract*, first published in 1762. Yet, 260 years later, the wealthy few have amassed so much power that they have gained enormous influence over who is elected and what these officeholders decide.[14] If we continue to allow inequalities to grow, our democracies are at risk of crumbling along with the rights and freedoms they are supposed to guarantee for *all*, not just a select few.

The massive inequalities that characterize our economic system are also fueling the alienation, disillusionment, and discontent that further threaten democracy.[15] Neoliberal ideology, which equates a person's worth with their ability to accumulate money, has permeated our personal lives, disenfranchising broad swathes of the population.[16] It has simultaneously fueled resentment toward the elite and toward a system that feels rigged. This has helped pave the way for social movements like the Yellow Vests in France, the

12. Mark Granovetter and Richard Swedberg, *The Sociology of Economic Life*, 3rd ed. (Boulder: Routledge, 2011).

13. Jean-Jacques Rousseau, *Du contrat social ou Principes du droit politique* (Paris: P. Pourrat Frères, Éditeurs, 1839), 93. Translation our own.

14. Julia Cagé, *The Price of Democracy: How Money Shapes Politics and What to Do about It* (Cambridge, MA: Harvard University Press, 2020).

15. Joseph E. Stiglitz, *The Price of Inequality: How Today's Divided Society Endangers Our Future* (New York: W.W. Norton, 2012).

16. Brown, *In the Ruins of Neoliberalism*; Michèle Lamont, "From 'Having' to 'Being': Self-Worth and the Current Crisis of American Society," *British Journal of Sociology* 70, no. 3 (2019): 660–707; Michèle Lamont, "Addressing Recognition Gaps: Destigmatization and the Reduction of Inequality," *American Sociological Review* 83, no. 3 (2018): 419–444.

Tea Party in the United States, and the election of populist leaders around the world who make scapegoats of refugees, immigrants, and minority groups.[17] Compounding this is the effect of new technologies and algorithms, which have fomented political polarization and spread disinformation, often for profit, thereby further destabilizing democracy.[18]

Allowing power imbalances to become so great that they undermine the stability and sustainability of our democratic, social, and economic systems is thus not only morally objectionable but also detrimental to all, even the most powerful. As Nobel Prize–winning economists Abhijit Banerjee and Esther Duflo point out, for the rich "to argue for a radical shift toward real sharing of prosperity"[19] would be in their own self-interest. Yet, the short-term attraction of making ever more money often blinds the powerful to the long-term consequences of reinforcing massive imbalances in a social system in which we are all interdependent.[20]

Overall, the pristine power of unregulated markets—neoliberal utopia—has failed to deliver shared prosperity. Beyond the threats to democracy that it has generated, neoliberal capitalism's focus on financial value maximization with little regard for the environmental implications of such a quest has also accelerated the deterioration of the planet and its ecosystems.[21] This threatens all of humanity, but people in the Global South, Indigenous populations, and socially and economically disadvantaged groups in the North bear the greatest risk.[22] The past decade has been the hottest on record, triggering wildfires, severe storms, heat waves, and the melting of the Arc-

17. Abhijit V. Banerjee and Esther Duflo, *Good Economics for Hard Times* (New York: Public Affairs, 2019); Arlie R. Hochschild, *Strangers in Their Own Land* (New York, New Press, 2018); Pierre Rosanvallon, *Le siècle du populisme* (Paris: Le Seuil, 2020).

18. Cass R. Sunstein, *#Republic: Divided Democracy in the Age of Social Media* (Princeton, NJ: Princeton University Press, 2017); for a full review of the nuanced literature on social media and democracy, see Joshua A. Tucker et al., "Social Media, Political Polarization, and Political Disinformation: A Review of the Scientific Literature," Hewlett Foundation, March 2018. Accessed September 2021, https://ssrn.com/abstract=3144139.

19. Banerjee and Duflo, *Good Economics*, 256.

20. Battilana and Casciaro, *Power, for All*.

21. Naomi Klein, *This Changes Everything: Capitalism vs. the Climate* (New York: Simon and Schuster, 2014).

22. See John C. Dernbach et al., "Sustainability as a Means of Improving Environmental Justice," *Journal of Environmental and Sustainability Law* 19, no. 1 (2012): 3–34; and US EPA, *Climate Impacts on Human Health* (2017). Accessed September 2021,

tic at an unprecedented speed.[23] Without fundamental societal and systemic transitions and transformations, the likelihood that Earth will suffer irreversible damage continues to increase.[24] Tellingly, researchers have found that over 70 percent of global greenhouse gas emissions from 1988 to 2015 were caused by just one hundred companies.[25] Unchecked corporate behavior, motivated solely by profit maximization, is careening us toward climate catastrophe.

The neoliberal model has reached a breaking point. Staying the course is untenable. Some citizens, especially members of younger generations, have taken up the critical fight for decisive action on climate change. Others have banded together to help preserve and expand our democracy by fighting for voting rights, protesting voter suppression, and calling for transparency in governance. To steer away from climate catastrophe and cultivate the soil of democracy, we must follow these examples of collective action to challenge the vast power differentials that persist in our politics and workplaces. If we fail to rebalance power among workers, top executives, and capital investors in companies and fail to hold companies accountable for not only their financial but also their social and environmental performance, our attempts at saving democracy and the planet will fall short.

https://19january2017snapshot.epa.gov/climate-impacts/climate-impacts-human-health_.html.

23. Bill McKibben, "Where We Stand on Climate," *New Yorker*, December 11, 2020, Accessed September 2021, https://www.newyorker.com/news/annals-of-a-warming-planet/where-we-stand-on-climate; Katherine Wu, "The 2010s Were the Hottest Decade on Record. What Happens Next?" *Smithsonian Magazine*, January 16, 2020. Accessed September 2021, https://www.smithsonianmag.com/smart-news/2019-was-second-hottest-year-record-what-now-180973995/.

24. For more on the potential of such fundamental societal and system transitions to mitigate the damage caused by climate change, see IPCC, "Summary for Policymakers," in *Global Warming of 1.5°C. An IPCC Special Report on the Impacts of Global Warming Of 1.5°C above Pre-Industrial Levels and Related Global Greenhouse Gas Emission Pathways, in the Context of Strengthening the Global Response to the Threat of Climate Change, Sustainable Development, and Efforts to Eradicate Poverty*, V. Masson-Delmotte et al. (Geneva, Switzerland: World Meteorological Organization, 2018).

25. It is important to note that in the top one hundred companies included in this finding of the CDP's and the Climate Accountability Institute's 2017 Carbon Majors report, a number of the companies are actually state-owned government enterprises. Furthermore, the percentage includes emissions associated with the sale of fossil fuels to consumers, and the consumers' subsequent use of those fossil fuels and associated emissions, in addition to emissions from extraction; Paul Griffin, *The Carbon Majors Database: CDP Carbon Majors Report 2017* (London: CDP, 2017), 14.

Rebuilding as a Fairer, More Democratic, and Greener Society

In March 2020, the COVID-19 pandemic reached American shores. Not only was it a human tragedy, but the pandemic was also a litmus test for and a crisis of inequality, revealing and reinforcing it simultaneously. As Adelle Blackett (p. 67) and Neera Chandhoke (p. 91) discuss in their chapters, the pandemic has had an outsized impact on people living in precarious situations, including in particular racialized groups around the world, informal workers, and migrants. And among these populations, as Imge Kaya-Sabanci underlines in her chapter, women have had to endure even more (p. 61). In the United States, 2.3 million women left the labor force between February 2020 and February 2021 (compared with 1.8 million men).[26] Unemployment among women aged twenty and older had doubled by the end of 2020, with the unemployment rate among Black and Latinx women both significantly higher than the unemployment rate among white men.[27] By early 2021, while life expectancy had fallen a full year overall, it fell by two to three years for Black and Latinx populations, reversing ten years of progress in closing the Black-white life expectancy gap.[28]

This is not only a health crisis but an economic and social one characterized by rising inequalities on top of an environmental crisis that has been ongoing for decades and now threatens life on Earth as we know it.[29] While the situation is undeniably alarming, we know from both experience and research that deep crises like these can facilitate change.[30] There will be a "before" and an "after" COVID.

---

26. Jonathan Rothwell and Lydia Saad, "How Have U.S. Working Women Fared during the Pandemic?" *Gallup*, March 8, 2021. Accessed September 2021, https://news.gallup.com/poll/330533/working-women-fared-during-pandemic.aspx.

27. Claire Ewing-Nelson, *All of the Jobs Lost in December Were Women's Jobs*, National Women's Law Center, Fact Sheet, January 2021. Accessed September 2021, https://nwlc.org/wp-content/uploads/2021/01/December-Jobs-Day.pdf.

28. Theresa Andrasfay and Noreen Goldman, "Reductions in 2020 US Life Expectancy Due to COVID-19 and the Disproportionate Impact on the Black and Latino Populations," *Proceedings of the National Academy of Sciences* 118, no. 5 (2021).

29. "UN Climate Warning: Immediate Change Needed to Preserve 'Life as We Know It,'" *World from PRX*. Accessed September 2021, https://theworld.org/stories/2018-10-08/un-climate-warning-immediate-change-needed-preserve-life-we-know-it.

30. Julie Battilana, Bernard Leca, and Eva Boxenbaum, "How Actors Change Institutions: Towards a Theory of Institutional Entrepreneurship," *Academy of Management Annals* 3, no. 1 (2009): 65–107; Neil Fligstein, "Social Skill and the Theory of Fields," *Sociological Theory* 19, no. 2 (2001): 105–125; Royston Greenwood, Roy Suddaby, and C. R. Hinings, "Theorizing Change: The Role of Professional Associations in the Transformation of Institutionalized Fields," *Academy of Management Journal* 45, no. 1 (2002):

The critical question to address is: What do we need to change to overcome the multidimensional crisis that confronts us? This is a colossal challenge. Constructing a society that is fairer, more democratic, and greener means breaking with existing power structures and the dominant norms of the neoliberal system. But circumstances demand that we rise to the occasion: the scale of the crisis we face requires radical change in our economic and social models. That, in turn, requires a collective effort from public authorities, social organizations, companies, and the scientific community as well as from each and every citizen. Herein lies the strength of collective movements: when people who seek change successfully organize across divisions to make demands in unison, they are able to overturn existing power structures and promote new norms.[31]

My research has shown that people's roles in collective movements for change can be divided into three categories: agitator, innovator, and orchestrator.[32] Agitators *speak out* against the status quo and raise public awareness of a problem. Today's young climate activists are a good example. Innovators *develop alternatives* to the status quo, proposing concrete avenues for change in the form of social or legislative innovations, for example. Orchestrators *implement solutions*, ensuring the coordination and collaboration of all the parties involved so that solutions can be adopted. There must be people working in all three categories for a change to be successfully adopted. Without innovation, without concrete proposals for change, agitation never surpasses mere criticism. And, without orchestration, even the most innovative ideas may never succeed in actually changing the way things work. Those of us seeking change today must work together to agitate, innovate, *and* orchestrate.

The Manifesto

Our desire to act not only as agitators but also as innovators and orchestrators first drew Isabelle Ferreras, Dominique Méda, and me

---

58–80; Elisabeth S. Clemens and James M. Cook, "Politics and Institutionalism: Explaining Durability and Change," *Annual Review of Sociology* 25, no. 1 (1999): 441–466.

31. Battilana and Casciaro, *Power, for All*.

32. Julie Battilana and Marissa Kimsey, "Should You Agitate, Innovate, or Orchestrate?" *Stanford Social Innovation Review*, 2017. Accessed September, 2021, https://ssir.org/articles/entry/should_you_agitate_innovate_or_orchestrate.

together to think about what we could do to help put human beings and the planet back at the heart of our economic system. Our mobilization effort began with the writing of an op-ed for the French newspaper *Le Monde* on the role and the importance of work during and after the pandemic. Initially, it was to be published on International Workers' Day, May 1, 2020. When the paper decided to publish it in mid-May instead, in a special issue on the world postlockdown, it gave us two weeks to circulate the text among colleagues in the academic community. All too aware that in many countries women experts' voices are often less represented in the public arena, we chose to share the text first with a group of female colleagues. These women, whose pioneering research provides concrete pathways to social and economic transformation, agreed to sign the op-ed and encouraged us to share it more broadly in the scientific community.

The enthusiasm the text generated surpassed our greatest expectations. It was quickly circulated beyond that initial group of women—who have since joined us as co-organizers of the initiative and coauthors of this book—to colleagues around the world. The op-ed resonated with researchers globally, who soon volunteered to translate it and orchestrate its release in their own countries. By the time it was published on May 16, the text had become a manifesto: it had garnered more than three thousand signatures from academics on five continents, representing a wide range of scientific disciplines, and had appeared simultaneously in twenty-three languages and forty-two national journals. At the same time that articles were being published across continents, volunteers helped us develop the initiative's website, www.democratizingwork.org, which features information about all signatories (now numbering more than six thousand), publishing newspapers, and available languages.

The Manifesto, which is reprinted in the following section of this book, starts with a critical question: What can the coronavirus crisis teach us? It then offers a simple answer: above all, human beings are more than mere resources. We must recognize the true value of each person's contributions. During the pandemic, those considered "essential workers" (including health-care workers, factory workers, delivery people, and supermarket cashiers, to name just a few) served on the frontlines, many without adequate protective supplies or even health-care coverage. Yet, they made it possible for others to quarantine and shelter in place. Their contributions are a testament to the importance of their work, but this work is too often undervalued and underpaid. Hence there is a stark discrepancy between the term *essential worker*, so rightly employed during this crisis, and the way our society actually values—or rather, undervalues—these workers' contributions. We must properly recognize each and every person's contributions at work and beyond.

Our manifesto is built on three pillars: *democratize firms*—give power and voice to employees so that they can participate in organizational decisions; *decommodify work*—ensure that work is not governed by market forces alone and that every person has the right to work; and, finally, *decarbonize our environment*—commit to preserving and protecting our natural ecosystems. These are the three levers we have at our disposal to make our societies of tomorrow fairer, more democratic, and greener.

Democratize, Decommodify, Decarbonize

The first lever of change, democratizing work, aims to share power more equitably, not only between shareholders and private owners but also with employees and those who have historically been, and continue to be, excluded from positions of power, such as women and racialized communities. One necessary (though not sufficient) first step entails reevaluating compensation by setting a higher minimum wage and by decreasing the gap between the highest-paid employees and those at the bottom of the pay scale. We must also protect workers from abuse, especially those made vulnerable by informal work arrangements or employment in the gig economy.[33]

Beyond these protections, employees must also have the power to participate in strategic decisions, working in partnership with their organization's executives and shareholders. The point here is not that they merely be allowed to express themselves, but that they be represented in the decision-making bodies of their companies, with the

---

33. Legislation like the PRO Act, which would strengthen the government's ability to punish employers who violate workers' rights, shield workers from retribution for attempting to unionize, and make it harder to classify workers as independent contractors to help ensure they received adequate benefits for their work, represents an excellent example of the sort of legislation that would help protect workers from abuse. See Nicholas Fandos, "House Passes Labor Rights Expansion, but Senate Chances Are Slim," *New York Times*, March 9, 2021. Accessed September 2021, https://www.nytimes.com/2021/03/09/us/politics/house-labor-rights-bill.html.

power to weigh in through both their voices and their votes. Numerous countries in Europe have laws that grant workers representation on their organizations' boards, in various levels and according to varying modalities, including Austria, Denmark, Norway, and Sweden.[34] Germany's system, called codetermination, is among the most advanced, having become dominant in the wake of World War II. Interestingly, however, according to legal expert Ewan McGaughey, the world's oldest codetermination law continuously in force did not originate in Europe. Instead, it dates back to April 1919, when Calvin Coolidge, the newly elected governor of Massachusetts, signed an act stating that a "manufacturing corporation may provide by by-law for the nomination and election by its employees of one or more of them as members of its board of directors."[35] Though rarely used, the act is still on the books today, in §23 of the Massachusetts Laws chapter on business corporations.

Overall, the democratization of firms requires that we shift from a model in which shareholders and executives monopolize decision-making power to one in which power is rebalanced and shared with employees. This will finally enable workers to gain control over decisions that directly affect their working lives and livelihood. In their contributions, Isabelle Ferreras (p. 23), Lisa Herzog (p. 55), Hélène Landemore (p. 47), and Sara Lafuente (p. 73) present and discuss the reasons for, and ways in which, this kind of power sharing could become a reality. Building on these arguments, Julia Cagé (p. 79) explains why democratization is particularly important for the media industry.

The second lever of change is the decommodification of work. Certain sectors, such as health care and education, must be protected from market logic and market forces. The pandemic offers a chilling illustration of what happens when the market alone decides: in the midst of an acute health crisis, millions of Americans had no health insurance. In addition to the thirty-one million Americans who were

---

34. Natalie Videbæk Munkholm, *Board Level Employee Representation in Europe: An Overview* (Brussels: European Commission Directorate General for Employment, Social Affairs and Inclusion, 2018).
35. Ewan McGaughey, "Democracy in America at Work: The History of Labor's Vote in Corporate Governance," *Seattle University Law Review* 42 (2019): 697–753. For the Massachusetts law, see https://malegislature.gov/Laws/GeneralLaws/PartI/TitleXXII/Chapter156/Section23 (accessed September 2021).

uninsured before COVID-19 hit, the first wave of pandemic-induced unemployment cost many Americans their paychecks and their health coverage.[36] Decommodifying work means that we must not let the so-called labor market decide our future. As noted above, those who hold more power in society—those with more resources—control the market. Far from apolitically distributing goods and services, the market is inherently political, as it is embedded in the power relations that make up human society. In fact, it is not only embedded within them; it replicates them. Relying on the labor market allows those who control it to decide everything. And when those who control it prioritize maximizing their financial returns, workers cease to be seen as human beings and become mere resources.

But decommodifying work goes beyond merely recognizing that something other than market forces is needed to regulate certain community needs. It means accepting that work is a right, not a commodity.[37] With the threat of unemployment still a significant risk to societies around the world in the aftermath of COVID-19, we must act to ensure that all people who seek a job have access to one that allows them to live with dignity and contribute to their communities. Pavlina Tcherneva's contribution (p. 85) proposes that this right be extended to all through a job guarantee and new training programs that would help foster innovative partnerships across the public, private, and nonprofit sectors. A number of job guarantee programs have already been piloted around the world to put this principle into action. In 2015, France launched an experiment called Zero Unemployment Territories, through which the state has incubated a series of companies whose core purpose is creating jobs. Subsidized by the state, they match a community's needs with the skills of those who are unemployed in that region, effectively providing employment while not taking jobs away from those who are already employed. Largely considered successful, the pilot is now expanding from ten regions to a minimum of sixty.[38] Isabelle Ferreras, in her chapter

---

36. David Blumenthal et al., "Covid-19: Implications for the Health Care System," *New England Journal of Medicine* 383, no. 15 (2020): 1483–1488.

37. Article 23 of the Universal Declaration of Human Rights (1948) recognizes the universal right to work: "Everyone has the right to work, to free choice of employment, to just and favourable conditions of work and to protection against unemployment."

38. "Loi du 14 décembre 2020 relative au renforcement de l'inclusion dans l'emploi par l'activité économique et à l'expérimentation territoire zéro chômeur de longue durée," *Vie Publique, Government of France.* Accessed September 2021, https://www

(p. 23), shows how the implementation of such programs aligns naturally with the project of democratizing firms.

The third and final lever of change is decarbonization, which Dominique Méda rightly argues will require an "environmental upshift." This transformation is so profound that it requires a radical shift in our mindset as well as deep industrial and organizational restructuring. We all have a role to play if we wish to preserve the environment and decarbonize the economy. As citizens and consumers, we undoubtedly must change our habits, but public authorities and businesses must also lead the way. States must implement stricter environmental legislation in coordination with global efforts. As for companies, they will have to shift away from carbon-heavy production, while some workers will need to migrate from more polluting to greener sectors of the economy.

This transition to a greener economy and society illustrates how the three principles, democratize, decommodify, and decarbonize, go hand in hand. We cannot decarbonize without guaranteeing a right to work to those who will bear the brunt of the transition to greener industries. Decommodifying helps ensure this urgent transition occurs, while also safeguarding the dignity of workers and fulfilling our two fundamental human needs for safety and self-esteem.[39]

As for democratizing, Alyssa Battistoni's contribution (p. 103) addresses the often-overstated tensions between empowering workers in ecologically destructive industries and decarbonizing, highlighting that unchecked corporate power is detrimental to both workers and Earth. She retraces the influential role of unions throughout US history in fighting for environmental protections as well as the potential for workers and communities in global supply chains to influence environmental standards of production in a democratized multinational firm. Democratizing companies will also help ensure that they can more effectively balance environmental and social concerns with financial ones. Cooperatives, like Sandra's, and social businesses, such as microcredit organizations and companies that recruit and hire the long-term unemployed, have led the way in broadening the definition of business objectives to include value beyond financial

.vie-publique.fr/loi/275990-loi-14-decembre-2020-extension-experimentation
-territoire-zero-chomeur.

39. Battilana and Casciaro, *Power, for All*.

returns. And my research has shown that companies managing to sustain the joint pursuit of financial, social, and environmental goals over the long term tend to adopt more democratic decision-making processes that engage their executives and shareholders as well as their employees.[40] Diverse points of view surface through these decision-making processes, helping companies better account for the social and environmental impacts of their decisions rather than just the financial implications.[41]

What Now?

The COVID-19 pandemic has been and continues to be a terrible tragedy. But it also represents a chance to change the way business is done. Governments—and the citizens they represent—now have more leverage than ever to change the business ecosystem, particularly through making their aid contingent on serious shifts in corporate goals and practices. National governments have an essential role to play in helping consumers and businesses in this transition. It falls to them to update legislation and public policy to better account for social and environmental value creation.

The three levers we present in this book—democratize, decommodify, decarbonize—are intended to inform our actions as we accelerate the transition process. In the pages immediately following the Manifesto, Isabelle Ferreras explores the significance of each of these levers and discusses the ways in which they are connected as well as how they can be implemented. All subsequent contributions start with a phrase from the Manifesto as a springboard to discussing one or more of these levers in connection with each author's research. They offer avenues for change while highlighting regional differences that will require adaptations to fit local constraints and

---

40. See Julie Battilana et al., "Les clés d'une gestion hybride réussie," *Harvard Business Review France* (August–September 2019): 67–75; and Julie Battilana, "La poursuite conjointe d'objectifs sociaux et financiers dans les entreprises. L'entreprise sociale comme laboratoire d'étude des modes d'organisation hybrides," *Entreprise and Société* 2, no. 4 (2019): 3–94.

41. Julie Battilana, Michael Fuerstein, and Matthew Lee, "New Prospects for Organizational Democracy? How the Joint Pursuit of Social and Financial Goals Challenges Traditional Organizational Designs," in *Capitalism Beyond Mutuality? Perspectives Integrating Philosophy and Social Science*, ed. Subramanian Rangan (Oxford: Oxford University Press, 2018).

opportunities. Our book closes with a reflection by Dominique Méda
that ties together the various themes of our work and invites us to
make a collective commitment to "ecological upshift," a necessary
step toward preserving "enduring conditions for authentically human life on this earth," in the words of philosopher Hans Jonas.[42]

Building on research in the social sciences, our mission is to lay
the groundwork for rethinking our economic and social models, to
spark debate, and to encourage new lines of research and concrete
action. We are not naive. Nor do we purport to have all the answers.
We know all too well that positive change is not inevitable; nor will it
come by protest alone. To change existing power structures, we must
not only agitate; we must innovate and orchestrate the change we
wish to see.[43] The current crisis is also an opportunity for renewal and
transformation. We cannot let it pass us by. We must return humanity and the planet to their rightful place in our social and economic
systems: at the center. Each of us has a role to play—as agitators, as
innovators, as orchestrators—in forging the path ahead.

---

42. Hans Jonas, *Principe responsabilité: Une éthique pour la civilisation technologique*
(Paris: Le Cerf, 1990), 11, translation our own.
43. Battilana and Casciaro, *Power, for All*.

MANIFESTO

Work. Democratize. Decommodify. Decarbonize.

On May 16, 2020, in the fifteen days preceding its publication, the following text was signed by more than three thousand academics[1] working in more than 650 academic institutions worldwide. It was published on May 16–17 in forty-three national news publications on five continents, including the following: Ambito *(Argentina),* The Guardian *(Australia),* De Morgen *(Belgium),* Le Soir *(Belgium),* La Folha de

1. In addition to the twelve contributors to this work, this op-ed was signed by thousands of academics, including the following: Elizabeth Anderson (University of Michigan), Thomas Piketty (EHESS-Paris School of Economics), Saskia Sassen (Columbia University), Noam Chomsky (University of Arizona), Axel Honneth (Columbia University), Katharina Pistor (Columbia), Eva Illouz (EHESS, Paris), JaYati Ghosh (Jawaharlal Nehru), Debra Satz (Stanford), Michele Lamont (Harvard), Susan Neiman (Einstein Forum), Albena Azmanova (University of Kent), Susan Silbey (MIT), Nancy Fraser (New School for Social Research), Chantal Mouffe (Westminster), Léa Ypi (London School of Economics), Lisa Wedeen (Chicago), Isabelle Berrebi-Hoffmann (CNRS-Cnam, Paris), Bea Cantillon (Antwerpen), Sakiko Fukuda-Parr (New School for Social Research), Valeria Pulignano (KULeuven), Sarah Song (UC Berkeley), Françoise Tulkens (UCLouvain, European Courts of Human Rights 1998–2012), Melanie Walker (University of the Free State, South Africa), Charles W. Mills (CUNY Graduate Center), Ingrid Robeyns (Utrecht), Tommie Shelby (Harvard), Rahel Jaeggi (Humboldt Universität Berlin), Brandon M. Terry (Harvard), Serene J. Khader (CUNY Graduate Center), Alison Jaggar (University of Birmingham, UK–University of Colorado at Boulder), Annabelle Lever (Sciences Po-Paris), Isabelle Martin (Montréal), Dani Rodrik (Harvard University), William Sewell (Chicago), Gabriel Zucman (UC Berkeley), Rainer Forst (Frankfurt), James K. Galbraith (University of Texas-Austin), Peter Hall (Harvard), Frederic Vandenberghe (Universidade Federal do Rio de Janeiro), Tim Jackson (CUSP-Surrey), Benjamin Sachs (Harvard), Pablo Servigne (in-Terre-dependent researcher), Loïc Blondiaux (Université Paris 1 Panthéon-Sorbonne), Jean Jouzel (Académie des Sciences, France), Scott Viallet-Thévenin (Université Mohammed VI Polytechnique), Sophie Weerts (Lausanne), Alberto Alemanno (HEC Paris-NYU Law), Philippe Askénazy (CNRS-Paris School

Sao Paulo *(Brazil)*, Diario y Radio de la Universidad de Chile *(Chile)*, Made in China Journal *(China)*, A2larm *(Czech Republic)*, Politiken *(Denmark)*, Pressenza *(Ecuador)*, Delfi *(Estonia)*, Helsingin Sanomat *(Finland)*, Le Monde *(France)*, Die Zeit *(Germany)*, Epohi *(Greece)*, South China Morning Post *(Hong Kong)*, Stundin *(Iceland)*, The Wire *(India)*, Meidaan *(Iran)*, Davar *(Israel)*, Il Manifesto *(Italy)*, As-Safir Al-Arabi *(Lebanon)*, Média24 *(Morocco)*, Lakome2 *(Morocco)*, De Groene Amsterdammer *(The Netherlands)*, Klassekampen *(Norway)*, El Comercio *(Peru)*, Disonancia *(Peru)*, Gazeta Wyborcza *(Poland)*, Krytyka Polityczna *(Poland)*, Diário de Notícias *(Portugal)*, Publico *(Spain)*, El Diario *(Spain)*, La Vanguardia *(Spain)*, Le Temps *(Switzerland)*, La Presse *(Tunisia)*, Assahafa *(Tunisia)*, Barr al Aman *(Tunisia)*, Cumhuriyet *(Turkey)*, The Guardian *(United Kingdom)*, La Diaria *(Uruguay)*, The Boston Globe *(United States)*.

Working humans are so much more than "resources." This is one of the central lessons of the current crisis. Caring for the sick; delivering food, medication, and other essentials; clearing away our waste; stocking the shelves and running the registers in our grocery stores— the people who have kept life going through the COVID-19 pandemic are living proof that work cannot be reduced to a mere commodity. Human health and the care of the most vulnerable cannot be governed by market forces alone. If we leave these things solely to the market, we run the risk of exacerbating inequalities to the point of forfeiting the very lives of the least advantaged. How to avoid this unacceptable situation? By involving employees in decisions relating

of Economics), Aurélien Barrau (CNRS and Université Grenoble-Alpes), Neil Brenner (Harvard), Craig Calhoun (Arizona State University), Ha-Joon Chang (Cambridge), Erica Chenoweth (Harvard University), Joshua Cohen (Apple University, UC Berkeley, *Boston Review*), Philippe Van Parijs (UCLouvain), Christophe Dejours (CNAM), Olivier De Schutter (UCLouvain, UN Special Reporter on extreme poverty and human rights), Elaine Unterhalter (University College London), Archon Fung (Harvard University), Stephen Gliessman (UC Santa Cruz), Hans R. Herren (Millennium Institute), Sanford Jacoby (UCLA), Pierre-Benoit Joly (INRA—National Institute of Agronomical Research, France), Lawrence Lessig (Harvard University), Margaret Somers (Michigan), Ewan McGaughey (King's College London), David Marsden (London School of Economics), Jan-Werner Müller (Princeton), Gregor Murray (Montréal), Steven Vogel (UC Berkeley), Michel Pimbert (Coventry University, Executive Director of Centre for Agroecology, Water and Resilience), Raj Patel (University of Texas), George Steinmetz (Michigan), Laurent Thévenot (EHESS), Nadia Urbinati (Columbia), Jean-Pascal van Ypersele (UCLouvain), Judy Wajcman (London School of Economics), Sandra Laugier (Paris 1 Panthéon-Sorbonne), Hartmut Rosa (Friedrich Schiller University, Jena), and thousands of others. A complete, updated list is available at https://democratizingwork.org/.

to their lives and futures in the workplace—by democratizing firms. By decommodifying work—by collectively guaranteeing useful employment to all. As we face the monstrous risk of the pandemic and environmental collapse, making these strategic changes would allow us to ensure the dignity of all citizens while marshalling the collective strength and effort we need to preserve our life together on this planet.

Why democratize? Every morning, men and women, especially members of racialized communities, migrants, and informal economy workers, rise to serve those among us who are able to remain under quarantine. They keep watch through the night. The dignity of their jobs needs no other explanation than that eloquently simple term *essential worker*. That term also reveals a key fact that capitalism has always sought to render invisible with another term, *human resource*. Human beings are *not* one resource among many. Without labor investors, there would be no production, no services, no businesses at all.

Every morning, quarantined men and women rise in their homes to fulfill from afar the missions of the organizations for which they work. They work into the night. To those who believe that employees cannot be trusted to do their jobs without supervision, that workers require surveillance and external discipline, these men and women are proving the contrary. They are demonstrating, day and night, that workers are not one type of stakeholder among many: they hold the keys to their employers' success. They are the core constituency of the firm, but are, nonetheless, mostly excluded from participating in the government of their workplaces—a right monopolized by capital investors.

To the question of how firms and how society as a whole might recognize the contributions of their employees in times of crisis, democracy is the answer. Certainly, we must close the yawning chasm of income inequality and raise the income floor—but that alone is not enough. After the two World Wars, women's undeniable contribution to society helped win them the right to vote. By the same token, it is time to enfranchise workers.

Representation of labor investors in the workplace has existed in Europe since the close of World War II through institutions known as work councils. Yet, these representative bodies have a weak voice at best in the government of firms and are subordinate to the choices of the executive management teams appointed by shareholders. They have been unable to stop or even slow the relentless momentum of self-serving capital accumulation, ever more powerful in its destruction of our environment. These bodies should now be granted similar rights to those exercised by boards. To do so, firm governments (that is, top management) could be required to obtain dual majority approval, from chambers representing workers as well as shareholders. In Germany, the Netherlands, and Scandinavia, different forms of codetermination (*Mitbestimmung*) put in place progressively after World War II were a crucial step toward giving a voice to workers— but they are still insufficient to create actual citizenship in firms. Even in the United States, where worker organizing and union rights have been considerably suppressed, there is now a growing call to give labor investors the right to elect representatives with a supermajority within boards. Issues such as the choice of a CEO, setting major strategies, and profit distribution are too important to be left to shareholders alone. A personal investment of labor, that is, of one's mind and body, one's health—one's very life—ought to come with the collective right to validate or veto these decisions.

Why decommodify? This crisis also shows that work must not be treated as a commodity, that market mechanisms alone cannot be left in charge of the choices that affect our communities most deeply. For years now, jobs and supplies in the health sector have been subject to the guiding principle of profitability; today, the pandemic is revealing the extent to which this principle has led us astray. Certain strategic and collective needs must simply be made immune to such considerations. The rising body count across the globe is a terrible reminder that some things must never be treated as commodities. Those who continue arguing to the contrary are imperiling us with their dangerous ideology. Profitability is an intolerable yardstick when it comes to our health and our life on this planet.

Decommodifying work means preserving certain sectors from the laws of the so-called free market; it also means ensuring that all people have access to work and the dignity it brings. One way to do this is with the creation of a job guarantee. Article 23 of the Universal Declaration of Human Rights reminds us that everyone has the right to work, to free choice of employment, to just and favorable conditions of work, and to protection against unemployment. A job guarantee would not only offer each person access to work that allows them to live with dignity, it would also provide a crucial boost to our collective capability to meet the many pressing social and environmental challenges we currently face. Guaranteed employment would allow governments, working through local communities, to provide dignified work while contributing to the immense effort of fighting environmental collapse. Across the globe, as unemployment skyrockets, job guarantee programs can play a crucial role in assuring the social, economic, and environmental stability of our democratic societies. The European Union must include such a project in its Green Deal. A review of the mission of the European Central Bank so that it could finance this program, which is necessary to our survival, would give it a legitimate place in the life of each and every citizen of the EU. A countercyclical solution to the explosive unemployment on the way, this program will prove a key contribution to the EU's prosperity.

Environmental remediation. We should not react now with the same innocence as in 2008, when we responded to the economic crisis with an unconditional bailout that swelled public debt while demanding nothing in return. If our governments step in to save businesses in the current crisis, then businesses must step in as well and meet the general basic conditions of democracy. In the name of the democratic societies they serve, and which constitute them, in the name of their responsibility to ensure our survival on this planet, our governments must make their aid to firms conditional on certain changes to their behaviors. In addition to hewing to strict environmental standards, firms must be required to fulfill certain conditions of democratic internal government. A successful transition from environmental destruction to environmental recovery and regeneration will be best led by democratically governed firms in which the voices of those who invest their labor carry the same weight as those who invest their capital when it comes to strategic decisions. We have had more than enough time to see what happens when labor, the planet, and capital gains are placed in the balance under the current system: labor and the planet always lose.

Thanks to research from the University of Cambridge Department of Engineering (Cullen, Allwood, and Borgstein, *Environmental*

Science & Technology 45 (2011): 1711–1718), we know that "achievable design changes" could reduce global energy consumption by 73 percent. But . . . those changes are labor intensive and require choices that are often costlier over the short term. So long as firms are run in ways that seek to maximize profit for their capital investors alone and in a world where energy is cheap, why make these changes?

Despite the challenges of this transition, certain socially minded or cooperatively run businesses—pursuing hybrid goals that take financial, social, and environmental considerations into account and developing democratic internal governments—have already shown the potential of such positive impact.

Let us fool ourselves no longer: left to their own devices, most capital investors will not care for the dignity of labor investors; nor will they lead the fight against environmental catastrophe. Another option is available. **Democratize firms; decommodify work; stop treating human beings as resources so that we can focus together on sustaining life on this planet.**

5/16/2020

FROM THE POLITICALLY IMPOSSIBLE TO THE POLITICALLY INEVITABLE

Taking Action

ISABELLE FERRERAS

In the beginning of 2020, the lockdown orders issued by governments to help contain the spread of COVID-19 sparked an economic crisis of unprecedented scale. The pandemic and the crisis it caused have taken a disproportionate toll on the lives of the elderly and of people in precarious and poorly paid lines of work, particularly service workers, among whom women and racialized populations are overrepresented.[1] The death toll in the Black, Indigenous, and Latinx communities of the United States is a particularly shocking illustration of this fact.

In June 2020, world health leaders confirmed that human activity was responsible for the transmission of illnesses such as COVID-19 from animals to humans, throwing into stark light the degree to which our ecosystem has been degraded, threatened from all sides. "Nature is currently declining globally at rates unprecedented in human history," they reminded us once again. "We must recognize that the way we currently produce and consume food, and our blatant

---

1. Dominique Méda, "Les plus forts taux de surmortalité concernent les travailleurs essentiels," *Le Monde*, May 23, 2020.

disregard for the environment more broadly, has pushed the natural world to its limits."[2]

At the same time, in May and June 2020, the words "no justice, no peace" rang out through the streets of Minneapolis and from cities all around the world as protestors wearing protective masks to respect health precautions gathered in support of the Black Lives Matter movement and to speak out against the murder of yet another Black man under the knee of a white police officer. *Si vis pacem, cole justitiam.* If you want peace, cultivate justice. These words have been the ILO's motto for over a century now. Today, even louder, the ideals of environmental justice, social justice, and peace are calling us to apply them—together—as fundamental principles if we are to survive together on this planet. Will we finally hear?

What Have We Done with Those Principles?

"Whereas universal and lasting peace can be established only if it is based upon social justice . . ." These words open the preamble to the constitution of the International Labour Organization, founded in 1919 as part of the Treaty of Versailles, which ended World War I. A few decades later, in May 1944, at the close of World War II, the ILO's Philadelphia Declaration went on to affirm that "labor is not a commodity." And just over three years after that, the United Nations General Assembly adopted the Universal Declaration of Human Rights, whose first article states that "all human beings are born free and equal in dignity and rights." Written at the close of two particularly dark periods of human history, these texts are precious evidence that global crises can push us to embrace what once seemed impossibly lofty ideals as fundamental principles—in this case, the

---

2. Lizzy Rosenberg, "World Health Leaders: 'Human Activity to Blame for Diseases Like COVID-19,'" World Economic Forum COVID-19 Action Platform, June 23, 2020. Accessed September 2021, https://www.weforum.org/agenda/2020/06/the-un-who-and-wwf-believe-emerging-infectious-diseases-are-driven-by-human-activities/. See also the op-ed signed by representatives of the United Nations, the World Health Organization, and the World Wildlife Fund, which appeared in *The Guardian* on June 17, 2020. See also Adam Tooze, *Shutdown: How Covid Shook the World Economy* (London: Allen Lane, 2021). For more on planetary boundaries, see Will Steffen et al., "Planetary Boundaries: Guiding Human Development on a Changing Planet," *Science* 347, no. 6223 (2015), as well as the "ecological ceiling" and the "social foundations" that Kate Raworth proposes in *Doughnut Economics: Seven Ways to Think Like a 21st-Century Economist* (Hartford, VT: Chelsea Green Publishing, 2017).

ideal of world peace built on the bedrock of social justice—and even to enshrine them in international treaties.

At the very dawn of the ecological crisis now buffeting us on every continent and at every season, another ideal was enshrined by an international framework: the connection between social and environmental justice, which was made explicit at the first United Nations Conference on the Human Environment in June 1972. Its first principle declared that human beings bear "a solemn responsibility to protect and improve the environment for present and future generations." The text continues, "In this respect, policies promoting or perpetuating apartheid, racial segregation, discrimination, colonial and other forms of oppression and foreign domination stand condemned and must be eliminated." Two decades later, the Rio Declaration reaffirmed this link, opening with a recognition of "the integral and interdependent nature of Earth, our home" and proclaiming in Article 1 that "human beings are at the center of concerns for sustainable development. They are entitled to a healthy and productive life in harmony with nature." Nearly half a century closer to the zenith of this crisis, isn't it time we did more than acknowledge our ideals as fundamental principles? Isn't it time we finally acted on them?

Return to the Democratic Project

This crisis is an opportunity for us to stop and notice that, to an alarming degree, power over the fate of working humans and life on Earth is in the hands of two institutions: the first is what economists call the "labor market,"[3] and the other is corporations. These institutions and the extractive worldview that drives them—treating workers like traded commodities, extracting profits for capital investors— structure our existence and, in particular, our working lives. Their power and their reach threaten our equality *in dignity and rights* as well as our shared existence on this planet. This is a depressing observation, but this period of crisis should remind us that there is hope, too: crises can generate the urgency we need to radically change this state of affairs. Work, the uncomfortable meeting place of capitalism

---

3. Quotation marks are used here to underline the ways in which this expression is problematic, built as it is on the assumption, which we oppose, that human beings (or their labor) can be transformed into a commodity that is exchanged in markets.

and democracy, holds immense subversive power—enough power to change the world order.[4]

Work in "capitalist democracies" is a contradictory experience because capitalism and democracy are two different forms of government that distribute rights in dramatically different ways.[5] Capitalism grants political rights—specifically, the right to govern—to property owners (i.e., shareholders), while democracy grants political rights to all people, based on the ethical commitment to recognize and treat each other as equals. In a democratic society, political entities are run according to this democratic ideal. In a capitalist economy—even one functioning under the aegis of a political democracy—firms are run according to the capitalist principle of political power allocation. Workers have no political rights to govern the firm, despite the fact that these firms govern the everyday lives of their workers. Whether we are accustomed to thinking of democracy as a system of government or as a way of life, firms are undemocratic political entities, exercising untransparent and often unchecked control over the lives of their workers. The contradiction between people's expectations of equality in the greater community and the subordination they experience at work is so intense that for many workers it verges on the autocratic: indeed, philosopher Elizabeth Anderson describes workers as *subjects* of their corporate *dictators*.[6] If unchecked, the subordination companies demand from workers is only likely to grow as corporations' political power within nations and across the world continues to expand. There are two possible roads out of this contradiction: one is to *deepen and expand democracy*[7] into the economic realm by democratizing capitalism. The other one is to scrap the rules of democracy altogether, even in the political realm, and replace them with the rules of capitalism. This perilous second road

4. See Isabelle Ferreras, *Gouverner le capitalisme? Pour le bicamérisme économique* (Paris: Presses Universitaires de France, 2012) and Isabelle Ferreras, *Firms as Political Entities Saving Democracy through Economic Bicameralism* (Cambridge, UK: Cambridge University Press, 2017).

5. Joshua Cohen and Joel Rogers, *On Democracy. Toward a Transformation of American Society* (New York: Penguin Books, 1983).

6. Elizabeth Anderson, *Private Government: How Employers Rule Our Lives and Why We Don't Talk about It* (Princeton, NJ: Princeton University Press, 2017).

7. For more on this, see the work of Erik Olin Wright, who considered the democratic project from a dynamic perspective as a project to "deepen and extend" the principle of equality. Erik Olin Wright, *Envisioning Real Utopias* (London: Verso 2010), 240.

was the one the United States had been traveling until Joe Biden was sworn in as president in January 2021—which may merely put the brakes on this trend for a while, or may be the moment we finally change course; only the future will tell. We as societies have a choice: it *is* possible to replace the extractive worldview that currently dominates our understanding of work with a democratic and sustainable model of work and the economy.

As John Dewey argued, democracy is much more than just a system of government.[8] The goal of democracy is to transform into action the principle that all human beings, in all areas of society, are equal *in dignity and rights*. The actions taken in pursuit of this principle are part of an ongoing project, a "living experiment." Democracy, understood in this way, is better described as an ever-evolving set of practices than as a fixed system defined by a set of institutions. The representative and participatory institutions we build must be periodically reexamined to ensure they reflect the heart of our democratic culture, which is deep respect for the equal dignity of all—that they do indeed constitute a government *of* the people, *by* the people, and *for* the people. If our institutions are to keep pace with the living culture of democracy, if we are to effectively and actively uphold the ideal of equality for all, then they must regularly be revised and improved. This, today, means reexamining the institutions that govern our work lives, which absorb the bulk of our hours and days. After the World Wars, the international institutions I mentioned in the opening paragraphs of this chapter acknowledged the principle of equal dignity for all, in all places. The recognition of this principle was accompanied, in many countries in the West, by a recognition of workers' essential contributions to the war effort at the national level. These governments extended citizenship to women generally and into the workplace specifically to further the democratic project and deepen democratic culture. This acknowledgment of our equality in dignity and rights enabled unprecedented numbers of workers to enjoy unprecedented levels of voice. This expansion was often described as a move toward "industrial citizenship." In most European countries, worker representation in firms was institutionalized in works councils. In Germany, the system of codetermination was established in the coal and steel industries, requiring company

8. John Dewey, *The Ethics of Democracy* (Ann Arbor: Andrew and Company, 1888).

boards to have equal numbers of representatives for workers and capital investors. These were concrete translations of the ideal of equality *in dignity and rights* into rights that helped ensure that all human beings had a say in collectively setting the norms and standards to which they were subject as individuals and as a collective.

It is time to honor that history, to continue the work it began. The solutions we propose here are offered at a time when the contradiction between democracy and capitalism has come to seem untenable, impossible, too intense to bear. We wrote these words together in the hope that we will remember that there is more than one road out and that, together, we *can* continue to deepen our democratic culture, we *can* keep finding new ways to translate our ideals into effective action—not just for those who invest the labor that brings companies and economies to life, but for the planet as well. These suggestions were not born in a vacuum. They have deep roots in the key principles our societies salvaged from the ashes of other tragedies. The men and women who set them down had weathered history's darkest hours with wisdom and clear-sightedness. In writing this book, we remember their drive to rekindle hope, to help light our way out of the shadows. We join the optimism of our will to theirs, drawing on their learning and adding to it with our own.

Recognize the Core Constituents of Firms

As the Philadelphia Declaration affirmed, work is not a commodity. It is an investment by those who perform it. It is not an investment as the term is used in economic discourse, which is to say, a quantified thing—in this case, time, skill, and effort—to be used as an instrument to obtain a desired external end or objective, usually one that was set or decided by a third party. Instead, work is an investment in the sense that the worker invests not just their skill, time, and effort, but their entire person—their intelligence, their emotions—in their labor as well as their care for and feelings toward coworkers or others as they go about their jobs. Cashier, crossing guard, courier, teacher, nurse, lawyer, doctor, or computer programmer: no matter how their job is perceived or remunerated, each person invests themself, their mental and physical health, in the work that they do. One would be hard-pressed to find a contemporary company that does not mention the value that this investment of intelligence, care, and emotion adds to the goods or services it offers. And yet, despite moments such as this COVID-19 crisis, when labor investment—even by workers who generally remain invisible because of the subaltern positions they hold—has been declared "essential," all interest in this critical investment somehow evaporates when it comes to recognizing workers' freedom and equal rights in the workplace. The organizations in which people's work lives unfold are governed solely by those who contribute capital to them—and, by comparison, the risk taken by capital investors is extremely limited: hence, the term *limited liability*.[9]

But while the risk taken by capital investors is restricted to the sum they originally invested, the risk borne by labor investors is not. This risk is coming to be recognized as a serious one and their "return on investment" as unfair when compared with that of capital investors.[10] We live in a world where it is only those who contribute capital to a firm, most often through the legal vehicle of the corporation, who have control over that firm's government.[11] With the rise of the platform economy, more and more corporations are deploying strategies aimed at denying employment relationships even the most basic protections and allowing capital investors to escape even the most basic responsibilities associated with the role of employer—what I call the *Reductio ad Corporationem*.[12] More and more, the lives of workers in the West are characterized by the same word that characterizes the lives of workers worldwide: *informality*. On the African continent, over 85 percent of jobs are informal; in Europe, the proportion has now climbed to over 25 percent.[13] Just as important, perhaps, these strategies aim to hide or distract from the

9. For more on this point, see Isabelle Ferreras, "Those Who Work Are Labor Investors," in *A Seat at the Table: Worker Voice and the New Corporate Boardroom* (Washington, DC: The Aspen Institute Business & Society Program Report Series, 2021). Accessed September 2021, https://www.aspeninstitute.org/wp-content/up loads/2021/08/Final-Worker-Voice-and-the-Corporate-Boardroom.pdf.

10. See Emmanuel Saez and Gabriel Zucman, *The Triumph of Injustice: How the Rich Dodge Taxes and How to Make Them Pay* (New York: W.W. Norton, 2019).

11. See the work of David Ellerman and Jean-Philippe Robé on the distinction, de facto and de jure, between the firm and the corporation.

12. See Ferreras, *Firms as Political Entities*.

13. "More than 60 per cent of the World's Employed Population Are in the Informal Economy," International Labor Organization, press release, April 30, 2018. Accessed September 2021, http://www.ilo.org/global/about-the-ilo/newsroom/news /WCMS_627189/lang--en/index.htm. See Neera Chandhoke's chapter in this volume.

firm's second core constituency, making democratization appear to be pointless and impractical. Yet this problem is due in large part to our failure to recognize labor as an *investment* in a shared undertaking, instead of a resource to be exploited: through their investment of labor in the firm, workers make up the firm's forgotten constituency, whether or not they benefit from the formal status of employee.

Ending the Race to the Bottom:
Collective Bargaining across the Value Chain

The Philadelphia Declaration of 1944 "recognizes the solemn obligation of the International Labour Organization to further among the nations of the world programmes which will achieve . . . the effective recognition of the right of collective bargaining." The invention of collective bargaining, born of the labor struggles at the turn of the twentieth century, produced a radical institutional innovation that made the ideal of democratizing and decommodifying work into a concrete possibility.[14] Despite its transformative potential, collective bargaining today has been weakened to the point that it is nearly forgotten by many. This is a dangerous omission, as collective bargaining recognizes the right of workers to a *collective* voice, represented by independent unions. When scaled up at the industry level (this is usually called "sectoral collective bargaining"), collective bargaining acknowledges that certain basic rights and conditions hold true across workplaces—that workers everywhere ought to be able to expect bathroom breaks, clean water, and safe workstations, for example. Instead of forcing workers and unions to exhaust themselves battling over contract conditions in one place, then another, and then yet another one, collective bargaining scales the setting of standards up to the level of an industry, a region, a sector, or some combination of these. Collective bargaining, conducted between union representatives chosen by workers and employers, at the level of a given industry—or even across an entire economy—is the most intelligent solution already at our disposal for today's work world to decommodify labor. It acknowledges that if workers are dispersed in

---

14. Beatrice and Sidney Webb, observing the actions of English workers at the turn of the twentieth century, were the first theorists of the radical innovation of collective bargaining and its democratic implications. Sidney Webb and Beatrice Webb, *Industrial Democracy* (London: Longmans, Green & Co, 1897).

many different workplaces and isolated in atomized work relation-ships, they will inevitably be corralled into a race to the bottom, selling their individual labor—meaning they will inevitably end up with little to no power in their relations with employers. At the same time, it is a highly efficient way for labor and management within a sector, an industry, or a region to work together to collectively set workplace standards that will attract and retain "talent;" that is, whatever type of workers those firms need. Organizing and collective bargaining are necessary conditions for the achievement of workers' equality *in dignity and rights* at an individual level, too.

Collective bargaining laid a cornerstone in a new democratic ar-chitecture of work relations. Why? It formally recognized that any economic endeavor is the result of the collective labor investment provided by workers and that this labor investment should be repre-sented, collectively, from the firm level up. Since the 1970s, however, collective bargaining has been plowed under in a concerted effort by capital-investor-driven corporations seeking to wrest power from labor investors. We must uncover this buried cornerstone and con-tinue building, for collective bargaining has the potential to shut the door on attempts by employers to establish highly imbalanced relationships between themselves and individual workers.

The path toward decommodification and democratization opened by the invention of collective bargaining is waiting to be extended across the globe, across entire industries, and into every company. Collective bargaining was forged from an ideal of solidar-ity among workers, and it should be prioritized as a tool first at the level of the global economy, then at national and regional levels, then within sectors or branches, and, ultimately, within each company. In practical terms, this means that a firm should not be able to negotiate employment terms and working conditions for workers that are less favorable than the standards negotiated at the upper levels (that is, sectoral, national, or international levels). This would immediately advance the goal of decommodifying work by fostering an economy in which employment and working conditions were negotiated in view of their *improvement* and in which businesses could no longer compete destructively by lowering pay or worsening working condi-tions. The expansion of collective bargaining would help companies move away from an extractive approach to human beings and their labor force, and from the dead end of "bargaining down." Rather than the current situation, in which those who contribute capital are able to collectively organize through the institution of the corporation while no equal institution exists for those who invest labor, collective bargaining would provide companies with the opportunity to focus *upward*[15] on strategies to improve the quality of their products and services and ways to stand out in terms of innovation capacity, quality, and the work experience of their labor investors.

The race to the bottom in terms of labor standards leads . . . to the bottom. We must take another road. Specifically, industry-wide or sectoral bargaining must be structured from a transnational perspective, taking into account the entire value chain so that all affected workers are included, even in transnational firms functioning across complex supply chains.[16] It must be expansive enough to reconnect the dots in firms whose "suppliers" actually stand in for production departments of their own so that these workers can be fully taken into account as the labor investors of those firms.

Beyond Distributive Justice: Political Rights

As many have said, we must flatten the wage curve. But distributive justice at the global and governmental scale is not enough to nurture a democratic and sustainable society. Along with raising wages and progressive tax reforms, *internal* democratic justice must extend the work of distributive justice into firms if true equal dignity among all humans is to be achieved at last. Both within and across national borders, the currently unequal distribution of wealth among firms' richest capital investors and the poorest labor investors would stand a far better chance at being corrected in democratized firms that include all of their constituents in their government—from workers sewing labels into garments (usually somewhere in the Global South), to sales associates in those labels' retail stores (most likely operating under franchise), all the way to the label designers (generally working in big cities in the Global North).

15. See the notion of the "*high road economy*" developed by Joel Rogers in Erik Olin Wright and Joel Rogers, *American Society: How It Really Works* (New York: W.W. Norton, 2015).

16. See Benjamin L. McKean, *Disorienting Neoliberalism: Global Justice and the Outer Limit of Freedom* (Oxford: Oxford University Press, 2020).

Societies cannot go on as they have. Organizations cannot go on as they have. The time has come for society as a whole and for companies in particular to recognize workers' contributions, especially those who, during the pandemic, showed just how essential they really are. And the same is true for the workers who stayed at home, shouldering the impossible mission of working remotely alongside children and family members sheltering with them, meeting the goals and targets of their organizations from home offices, dining tables, and repurposed living spaces. It is not enough to recognize these contributions with messages of gratitude broadcast over social media by more or less earnest internal communications departments. Truly acknowledging the magnitude of these contributions means deepening our understanding of labor and of citizenship. Maintaining our status as equals inside the workplace—continuing to be *equal in dignity and rights* as we go about our jobs—requires us as societies to recognize the political rights of labor investors to have a voice, not just in managing, but in governing their work lives.

Capitalist firms are political entities whose continued existence depends on two constituents, capital investors and labor investors. Currently, although businesses could not survive without labor investors, and while labor investors are the only constituency *governed* by the rules of the firm, the labor investors are nonetheless excluded from firm government (all other constituencies—capital investors, customers, local communities, etc.—are stakeholders who, while they may be affected by a firm's decisions, do not experience firms ruling their daily lives).[17] Workers should therefore be included as a constituency in the government of firms and should benefit from at least the same rights as those enjoyed by capital investors. Democratizing work injects the principle of collective bargaining into the very heart of companies in order for labor investors to have a collective voice in the ends as well as the means of their shared endeavor. What services should be provided? What products should be developed? Who should benefit from them? With what means? How can effort be fairly distributed? Who should be chosen as CEO? As we wrote

---

17. For more on the inalienable rights of workers, see the work of David P. Ellerman, *Neo-Abolitionism: Abolishing Human Rentals in Favor of Workplace Democracy* (Springer International Publishing, 2021).

in the Manifesto: "A personal investment of labor . . . ought to come
with the collective right to validate or veto these decisions."

Organizational Solutions—Past and Future

Abandoning the paradigm that sees and treats workers as instruments
("human resources") in favor of one that empowers them to weigh in
on the strategies of their firms requires that labor investors, like those
who contribute capital, be able to choose their own representatives.
As mentioned previously, in many European countries, institutional
bodies through which the collective voice of labor investors can be
expressed already exist. Known as works councils, these bodies
usually bring together worker representatives elected by workers
themselves from union slates. If they were considered as analogous
to boards of directors, these councils would have the potential to
function as one of the chambers in a two-chamber firm parliament.
Within the standard hierarchy of an organization, in other words,
this second chamber of labor representatives would function at the
same level of the board of directors. A dual majority—meaning a
majority in each chamber—would thus be required to approve the
appointment of a CEO as well as major decisions, such as the firm's
strategy, its pay scale, and the distribution of profits. The philosophical principle underlying this concept of government comes from
the history of political bicameralism, which made it possible to begin the process of democratizing political entities caught under the
despotic rule of one of their constituent groups. Put succinctly, it is
the principle of joint decision-making, with collective veto power for
each constituent group.[18]

   Organizationally speaking, applying the philosophical principle
of dual majority to the capital and labor investor constituents of firms
might happen in a number of ways. A second chamber could be established, or a single board of directors or supervisory board might be
expanded to include equal numbers of capital and labor representatives, requiring majority votes from each group.[19] The Manifesto

---

18. This idea might be seen as a deepening of the German practice of comanage-
ment (or codetermination), although dual majority model is a much more rigorous
mechanism. Sara Lafuentes's essay examines this difference (p. 73).
   19. Further development on this proposal in the US legal context: Sharon Block,
and Benjamin Sachs, "Clean Slate for Worker Power Report," *Harvard Labor and
Worklife Program* (January 2020): 71–73; and Julie Battilana and Isabelle Ferreras,

lays out the philosophical principle that should underpin the choice of institutional arrangement: "A personal investment of labor, that is, of one's mind and body, one's health—one's very life—ought to come with the collective right to validate or veto [a firm's] decisions." Logically, recognizing that labor investors are essential implies that they ought to have the power to collectively approve their firms' strategic decisions (or to reject them, as the case may be)–this *de facto* amounts to a collective veto power. Today, in corporate firms, this power remains solely in the hands of those who invest their capital, represented by the board of directors.

The collective veto power exercised by labor investors at the level of corporate governance is the institutional translation of what, in labor history, has sometimes been called *worker control* or *workplace democracy*. It is a transitional proposal and could serve as a bridge toward the complete democratization of firms via labor investors' buyback of shares in their firm from capital investors, helping expand the democratic model of the cooperative, democratic firm to the economy as a whole.[20] Democratic nations ought to ensure that a financial sector adapted to these potentially fully democratic firms exists to support this transition. The history of ESOPs (employee stock ownership plans) in the United States shows that true democratic conversion is a credible option while also revealing the severe limitations of democratization strategies that are based solely on property ownership. It should be very clear that the mechanism of the dual majority or double collective veto rights discussed here is distinct from *capitalist* democratization strategies that focus on access to property ownership. The right of workers to a collective say in decisions regarding their organizations should not be made contingent upon, and are not justified by, property ownership.[21]

"From Shareholder Primacy to a Dual Majority Board," in *A Seat at the Table: Worker Voice and the New Corporate Boardroom* (Washington DC: The Aspen Institute Business & Society Program Report Series, 2021): August, 25–30. Accessed September 2021, https://www.aspeninstitute.org/wp-content/uploads/2021/08/Final-Worker-Voice-and-the-Corporate-Boardroom.pdf.

20. On the proposal of economic bicameralism at the firm level as a "real utopia," see Isabelle Ferreras, Tom Malleson, and Joel Rogers, eds. *Democratizing the Corporation. The Proposal of the Bicameral Firm* (London: Verso, forthcoming).

21. This is precisely what is at stake in the project of democratization: to decouple the enjoyment of political rights from the possession of assets, be they real estate assets—as was the case of the British lords—or financial assets—as is the case with firm shareholders. We have made political advances throughout history along the lines of this delinking (Thomas Piketty, *Capital and Ideology* [Cambridge, MA: Harvard

Acknowledging that the right to a voice does not depend on ownership in no way excludes the possibility that workers and their representatives, having learned to govern their firms, might also buy back shares in their firms from capital investors through worker-governed trusts, thus collectively owning as well as running their firms. The point of this proposal is to open the door for a much broader range of democratically governed firms, including hybrid organizational structures,[22] self-managed organizations, cooperatives, commons, or other structures in which capital contributions do not automatically come with political rights but instead remain debts to be paid back collectively. This would be a new chapter in the history of democracy, one in which firms could at long last be included—providing that they meet the standard of guaranteeing that their workers have the right to collectively validate or veto those firms' strategic decisions. Companies with a robust commitment to democratic standards would develop more constructive relationships with governments and public powers, oriented by a co-constructed understanding of the common good rather than a desire to avoid or undermine democratic public powers or circumvent the norms intended to keep them in check, as is currently the case.

Unions built on the recognition of pluralism and the exercise of internal democracy are the best way to coordinate elected worker representatives.[23] Unions are the safeguards of the essential principle of "cross-company solidarity," as Georges Friedmann, the father of French labor sociology, called it. As such, they have historically played a role in fostering and promoting solidarity among workers spread across different firms. Only unions can ensure that bolstering

---

University Press, 2020]), but there are regressions underway (Julia Cagé, *The Price of Democracy* [Cambridge, MA: Harvard University Press, 2020]). From an operational perspective, the advance of the democratic project should be assessed in the light of our ability to unbundle political rights from the possession of property in the political realm and in the economic realm.

22. For more on hybrid organizations, see Julie Battilana, "La poursuite conjointe d'objectifs sociaux et financiers dans les entreprises. L'entreprise sociale comme laboratoire d'étude des modes d'organisation hybrides," *Entreprise & société* 2, no. 4 (2019): 53–94.

23. We could as easily imagine that these representatives be selected among workers via a sortition process using union-affiliated slates, calculated depending on the number of votes these slates garnered among the firm's workforce. See Hélène Landemore, *Open Democracy: Reinventing Popular Rule for the Twenty-First Century* (Princeton, NJ: Princeton University Press, 2020).

workers' rights within firms does not end up encouraging unhealthy forms of company patriotism or competition among workers in different companies. It should also be noted that all too often over the past three decades, initiatives grouped into the category of "corporate social responsibility" (CSR) have ended up diluting the constituent power of workers by drowning it in the ocean of stakeholders affected to varying degrees by corporate activities, unlike the firm's labor investors, who are not only affected but governed by the government of the corporation.[24] The result of this has been to further consolidate shareholder supremacy, distracting from any serious reflection on the specificities of labor investment by workers in firms. The philosophical principle of the right to collectively validate or veto the strategic decisions of the firm corrects this oversight, allowing the process of democratization to deepen within firms. Assuring that unions are optimally able to pursue their core functions, representing workers and maintaining robust solidarity among companies, economic sectors, and countries—as is the case in European works councils—is crucial if we wish to positively and radically transform national and international economies as well as our democracies.

Saying Goodbye to the Labor-Commodity Market

The COVID-19 crisis has shed stark light on the grave dysfunctions of our current labor market: despite a serious lack of nurses, for

24. CSR seeks to hold firms responsible for their actions and their impact on various groups of people. It is an approach based on the stakeholder theory of the firm, which considers all those involved in and impacted by the activities of a firm, including workers, suppliers, local communities, etc. In the summer of 2019, after forty years upholding the theory of shareholder primacy as promoted by the followers of Milton Friedman, the US Business Roundtable publicly embraced stakeholder theory. For more on why this shift is inadequate, see Isabelle Ferreras, "Shareholders vs Stakeholders: Lumping Workers in with Other Stakeholders Is a Euphemism that Obscures Reality," *Boston Review*, October 2019.

By contrast, as discussed earlier in this text, this manifesto affirms that labor investors are the excluded constituents of firm government. In so doing, we expand on a theory of the firm based on an understanding of the firm's dual constituencies pioneered by the German codetermination movement, whose logical next step is the principle of dual majority. See Ferreras, 2012, 2017, op. cit. For more on the differences between these theories, see also Christophe Clerc, "Report for ILO on Models of Corporate Governance (Vol. 1): Structure and Diversity of Corporate Governance Models" ("*Structure et diversité des modèles de gouvernement d'entreprise—Rapport pour l'Organisation internationale du travail*"), 2019. Available at SSRN, https://ssrn.com/abstract=3515477 or http://dx.doi.org/10.2139/ssrn.3515477.

example, salaries in the field have not risen commensurate with demand. Proponents of the so-called free market might be quick to declare that the market, stifled by too many regulations, was unable to naturally adapt price to demand. But the "market" is not where we should look in the first place to set the price of health care or determine a country's unemployment rate. Labor and health policy should be guided by the needs of our societies, not the fiction of a "natural" mechanism that is nothing more than the fruit of human choices and actions.

Using the term *labor market* to describe the context in which people circulate within the economic realm perpetuates the idea that work can be reduced to a commodity. As it is currently structured, the labor market is one in which some people are able to circulate freely while others are all but immobilized (think of the unemployed or of racialized and otherwise discriminated-against groups, for example). If we are to change the reality of the contemporary world of work, the so-called labor market must be transformed to the point that it will resemble something else entirely. Then and only then will the market be a place where people can circulate and coordinate freely among themselves, matching their talents to the work that needs them.

Consistent with such radical reform, it is crucial that public powers secure access for all to the basic goods required for a decent life. Alongside the right to employment, Articles 1, 22, 23, and 25 of the Universal Declaration of Human Rights affirm the right to education, housing, health care, and social security, including the right to unemployment and a decent retirement. As the pandemic has shown us, guaranteed access to quality health care is a key factor in assuring the future of our societies. Commodifying health care and linking it to individual employment status, as is the case in the United States, has proven to be an unfair model and a tragic choice for society's future. There is no justification for allowing the "labor market" to foster harmful competition among the weakest that forces people into an infernal race to the bottom, dragging down employment and labor conditions for everyone. All of this *could* cease—the time has come to make the decision that it *must* cease.

A protective floor should be put in place, set high enough to guarantee the provisions laid out in Article 23 of the Universal Declaration of Human Rights. With regard to labor policy, this is what a universal job guarantee would achieve.[25] Involuntary unemployment is a societal choice and an absurd one to make at a time when people's needs, and those of the planet, are so tremendous. As Pavlina Tcherneva explains in this book, a job guarantee would ensure that all those who wish to exercise their right to work under decent employment and labor conditions have access to a job. Employers seeking to fill jobs would either have to meet or exceed the conditions put in place by the job guarantee. A job guarantee, combined with working time reduction policies set at industry and national levels, would ensure that work's current grip on everyone's lives would not be stifling. Today, while some suffer from cruelly long hours, others lack opportunities to access decent and meaningful work. Sharing the collective pool of work hours will be beneficial to our collective well-being and to our environment, making lifestyles that are less consumption intensive more possible at the individual level. Perhaps even the *overworked American* Juliet Schor has described will finally find a little more time off the clock for life, liberty, and the pursuit of happiness.[26]

Protecting Labor Investors, Protecting Democracy

As Karl Polanyi observed more than half a century ago in his analysis of what pushed the German people to embrace fascism, when societies allow themselves to be organized by markets alone, the violence that those market relationships generate inside the social fabric intensifies to the point that it becomes unbearable. Sadly, this is an excellent description of what is occurring in our societies today: even before the COVID-19 pandemic struck, the election of xenophobic leaders such as Orban, Trump, and Bolsonaro was already evidence that this phenomenon was on the rise once again. Society, to summarize Polanyi's view, seeking to protect itself from the violence of the free market,[27] has already begun embracing political

25. See Pavlina Tcherneva, *The Case for a Job Guarantee* (London: Polity Press, 2020), as well as her contribution to this book (p. 85).

26. Juliet B. Schor, *The Overworked American: The Unexpected Decline of Leisure* (New York: Basic Books, 1993). See, for policy design and effects, Martin Pullinger, "Working Time Reduction Policy in a Sustainable Economy: Criteria and Options for Its Design," *Ecological Economics* 103 (July 2014): 11–19.

27. Karl Polanyi, *The Great Transformation: The Political and Economic Origins of Our Time* (Boston: Beacon Press, 2001 [1946]).

leaders that offer citizens distraction from the true causes of their problems by channeling anger toward various scapegoats (migrants, the European Union, Black people, Mexicans, Muslims, etc.). This destabilization of our political democracies will only continue if we do not take concrete action to decommodify work.

The principles of democratization and decommodification go together: building a solid floor for the "labor market" with a universal job guarantee will permit our societies to shape employment and labor conditions for the better and eradicate discrimination in *democratically run* firms. These are the solid foundations upon which we need to build a democratic architecture of collective labor relations at every level, from the company and the sector to the nation and the globe.

Protecting Labor Investors, Protecting the Planet

Throughout the course of history, significant advances in environmental protections have been made by including more people in decisions.[28] Today, the vast majority of workers are affected by environmental issues. A staggering number of these issues can be resolved through "low-tech," labor-intensive solutions, such as improving public transportation, renewing infrastructure, insulating buildings, diversifying systems for waste collection and treatment, and expanding the possibility for manufactured objects to be repaired—to name just a handful of examples.[29] With this observation in mind, it seems crucial to restate that within firm governments, people would be more closely aligned with the interests of the planet than institutions representing the needs of capital investors. Firm stakeholders such as local and regional governments, neighborhoods, or consumers are also a logical part of the dynamic of democratizing firms and should have voices within them, for example, through consultative positions in diversified works councils.

To link the last lever to the first two proposed by the Manifesto, a three-dimensional strategy—external, consultative, and internal—is

---

28. Valérie Chansigaud, *L'homme et la nature. Une histoire mouvementée* (Paris, Delachaux et Niestlé, 2015).

29. Jane McAlevey, *A Collective Bargain: Unions, Organizing, and the Fight for Democracy* (New York, Harper Collins, 2020).

needed.[30] First, it must be restated that external public action is urgently necessary to establish guidelines for safeguarding the planet, as the recent Citizens' Convention for Ecological Transition in France reminded us yet again. This includes but is not limited to setting the conditions for economic activity in every sector.[31] It is vital that our governments coordinate at the international level to impose strict environmental standards. These are a necessary framework so that negotiations between constituencies—labor investors and capital investors—in the democratized firms of the future are under no circumstances undertaken to the detriment of the planet. Individual firms should not be left to set their own environmental standards any more than they should be left to set their own labor standards.

Next, firms must commit to consulting with and informing stakeholder representatives (particularly consumers and local governments) concerned with their local and global environmental impact, and some of these consultations should be binding. In particular, representatives of relevant environmental organizations should be given a seat in bodies that resemble today's works councils or board committees, thus assuring them a right to information and consultation. In this way, they would remain in regular contact with the firm's top executives and would have to be consulted on significant environmental decisions.

Finally, it bears repeating that the government of firms *must* be transformed internally in a way that brings the extractive dynamic of capital interests to an end by changing the structure of the rights granted to those who invest capital.[32] As the Manifesto affirms,

30. Isabelle Ferreras, "Democratising Firms—A Cornerstone of Shared and Sustainable Prosperity," *CUSP Essay Series on the Morality of Sustainable Prosperity*, no. 10 (July 2019).

31. One realistic translation of this would be the application in every economic sector of the nine planetary boundaries identified by Rockström and Steffen, within which humanity can safely develop and thrive and whose crossing it is urgent to contain and reverse. Kate Raworth's theory of doughnut economics (*Doughnut Economics: Seven Ways to Think Like a 21st Century Economist* [New York: Random House Business, 2017]) provides one possible generalizable formulation. The European taxonomy underway (see work by the EU Technical Expert Group on Sustainable Finance) as well as other science-based targets can also help identify limits to be respected in each sector of the economy and could be used as the basis for binding external limits specific to activities in every economic sector, with criteria revised each year until every industry, and thus every sector of the economy, is functioning within these planetary boundaries.

32. See Thomas Piketty's discussion of firm governance in *Capitalism and Ideology* (Cambridge, MA: Harvard University Press, 2020). On the dynamics of rights

workers must exercise "the collective right to validate or veto [the] decisions" of firms, along with those who contribute their capital and who monopolize that power today. This power could be guaranteed to them by requiring a dual majority vote from the board to validate firm strategy. To be ratified, in other words, an organization's key decisions, in addition to approval by majority vote from the board of directors, as is the case today, would require approval by a majority from a body of worker representatives too. This could be organized by vesting works councils with veto powers in companies where they already exist or, in cases where they do not, by expanding boards of directors to include a special majority of labor investors' representatives.[33]

The link between the democratization and decommodification of work and the decarbonization and restoration of our environment cannot be overstated. Setting up a universal job guarantee would have immediate positive benefits in this direction. Legitimate fears, particularly of layoffs and unemployment, have fueled workers' objections to an ecological upshift, and a universal job guarantee would answer these fears with a concrete promise of new jobs, not only providing immediate and useful work but also easing the threat of long-term unemployment caused by the downgrading of their current professional skills. The remediation, renewal, and reconstruction needed to bring about the ecological upshift will need the full and creative support of our societies as they adapt to the many

---

associated with capital, their contingencies, and the possibilities to change them, see Katharina Pistor, *The Code of Capital: How the Law Creates Wealth and Inequality* (Princeton, NJ: Princeton University Press, 2020).

33. In the United States, which follows a monocameral model of firm government in which social and economic committees and works councils are unknown, a practical proposal for implementing this principle would be to establish a supermajority for elected labor representatives on company boards. See "Clean Slate for Worker Power. Building a Just Economy and Democracy," a report by Sharon Block and Benjamin Sachs, released in January 2020 by the Labor and Worklife Program at Harvard Law School, https://lwp.law.harvard.edu/files/lwp/files/full_report_clean_slate_for_worker_power.pdf. The practicalities of such reform in the United States could go from softer measures (such as providing tax incentives to corporations that put workers on their board and give them power in a meaningful way) as a way to incentivize firms to speed up their own democratization by giving them a justified competitive advantage, to more significant measures, such as legislative action to change structures of corporate governance at state and federal levels (pursuing the fruitful ideas of federal incorporation for large firms and federal licensing for firms incorporated at the state level engaging in interstate commerce).

unexpected ways in which climate devastation will continue to affect humanity.[34] Extreme pressure on agricultural systems and mass population displacements across the globe are already highly visible examples of this.[35]

High Technology Needs "Low-Tech" Solutions

We are at the very beginning of a new chapter of our history. If it is to continue—if humans are to survive the Anthropocene—we must learn to live together and create institutions capable of fostering mutual respect among human beings as well as respect for the other inhabitants, the boundaries, and the limitations of the biosphere of which we are a part. If we are able to accelerate the learning process required for this—that is to say, if we succeed in transforming our societies' relationship to work, as well as to all living communities, human and nonhuman—and, more broadly, if we come together to meet the sustainable development goals passed by the United Nations in 2015, then a democratic future is still possible. To this end, research in the social sciences is more important than ever. To return to the COVID-19 virus, and without calling into question the importance of vaccines or other technological advances, we have all seen what it really took to flatten the curve of infection: our safety has depended in large part on adapting our behaviors and social norms. In other words, it has depended on the institutions that preside over the organization of our lives together and which are the object of social science research. They are the source of our social resilience. Low-tech solutions such as hand-sewn masks (which might have made it possible to maintain sufficient supplies of disposable FFP2 masks for health-care workers), social distancing, changes in the way we interact, and other mitigation strategies—in short, our ability to transform our social norms—are just as important as technological advances.

Will technology save the planet? No. Rather, it is "soft" technologies—institutions, built on respect for all living beings and for our planet and its limits—that will make or break us in the end. Democratize,

---

34. See Elwyn de la Vega, et al., "Atmospheric CO_2 during the Mid-Piacenzian Warm Period and the M2 Glaciation," *Scientific Report* 10 (2020): 11002.

35. See Ionesco Dina, Daria Mokhnacheva, and François Gemenne, *Atlas Des Migrations Environnementales* (Paris: Presses de Sciences Po, 2016).

decommodify, decarbonize: these three principles, which inspired the thousands of researchers who signed this manifesto, may seem *politically impossible* for now, a far cry from our current realities. But at the same time, our societies have never been so close to making them *politically inevitable*, to borrow a phrase from . . . Milton Friedman.[36] Our survival depends on it.

In the pages that follow, before Dominique Méda's concluding chapter, ten female researchers will expand on a phrase or section of the Manifesto that connects with their own expertise, showing the many ways in which these three principles truly are "alive and available." Each of them has chosen a point in the Manifesto that particularly inspires them as a focal point for their own reflections and proposals. We live in a world where women face disadvantages on all fronts: women performing the same functions as men earn significantly less money; women possessing the same skills as men are less likely to be promoted to leadership positions. If we keep closing the global gender gap at the rate it has been narrowing between 2006 and 2020, it will take another 257 years to reach full equality.[37] The impact of the COVID-19 crisis, with its unprecedented combination of school closures and work from home, has disproportionally affected women, further increasing those inequalities. The shocking, disproportionate price paid by people of color and racialized communities in this crisis is just as alarming. Structural injustices such as these violate the fundamental commitment behind the Manifesto to the culture of democracy—to deeply respect all people as *equal in dignity and rights*. We felt that our specific responsibility at this moment in history was to fight

36. In his 1982 preface to *Capitalism and Freedom*, Milton Friedman (Chicago: University of Chicago Press, 1982) wrote that the "basic function" of academic researchers was "to develop alternatives to existing policies, to keep them alive and available until the politically impossible becomes politically inevitable." While our approach and our analyses could not be more different, I share Friedman's perspective on the role of research. Academic researchers have a crucial role to play in providing society with the tools it needs and in making them accessible and available. We should embrace fully this responsibility.

37. According to the *Global Gender Gap Report 2020* established by the World Economic Forum, 2019. To reference a few regions specifically: closing the gender gap would take 54 years in Western Europe, 59 years in Latin America, and 151 (!) years in North America (this is a reflection of the lack of progress in the region over the period of reference, 2006–2020). It should be borne in mind that this report was released before the COVID-19 crisis hit: the situation has only become worse since then.

against the invisibility of women, particularly in expert domains and in academia, and to help amplify the voices of woman scholars from around the globe.[38] For this volume, we have thus sought to reflect the strength and beauty of diversity across the globe with an all-female authorship.

Leaders of all kinds: elected officials, union leaders, entrepreneurs, journalists, artists, teachers, scholars, and scientists; labor investors and their organizations, unions, members of the labor movement as a whole; business actors, the cooperative business sector, essential workers, citizens of the world—right now, every one of us has choices to make. From one crisis to another, as we have observed over the past century, powerful basic principles, as *politically impossible* as they may once have seemed, have become inevitable to the point that they are now enshrined in our most important international treaties. There is no need to seek out new basic principles; rather, we must knit the ones we have together. In the past, the three principles laid out and explored in these pages inspired struggles that all too often took place in isolation from one another. A desirable future lies at the intersection of those struggles. Democratize, decommodify, decarbonize: we must undertake all three of them together, and work is the place where we can start this endeavor. The survival of humanity on a habitable Earth depends on it. The survival of the democratic project depends on it. One day soon, let us hope, we will look back and see that the *politically impossible* did indeed become *inevitable*.

38. Among those who signed the Manifesto, who were the potential contributors to this volume, we would like to thank our male colleagues, who were equally qualified to appear in this volume and who greeted this choice with such understanding and support.

DEMOCRATIZE FIRMS... WHY, AND HOW?

HÉLÈNE LANDEMORE

One question you may have asked yourself as you read the Manifesto is one that has shaped much of my working life: *Why* democratize? What makes it the best solution?

There are two sets of reasons for democratizing work, intrinsic and instrumental. Intrinsic reasons appeal to our intuitions about justice and workers' dignity, and in the end perhaps do not need much elaboration. The problem is that for people who do not share these intuitions about the worth of workers, intrinsic reasons might not suffice. By contrast, the instrumental case is causal and speaks to our rationality and interests. That is why I have chosen to focus on it before turning to the question of how we might begin to democratize firms.

Very briefly, though, let us examine the intrinsic reasons why we ought to democratize work. As the Manifesto points out, they have to do with the human dignity of workers, who are not mere human "resources," "capital," or "stock," although they are frequently given these kinds of labels. Workers are human and, as such, capable of self-rule, or autonomy, unlike inert firm inputs like capital or machinery. This autonomy (sometimes other sources of dignity are invoked but this is the more frequently mentioned) gives them the right to be respected.

Some proponents of democratizing work claim that all salaried work is a form of alienation and even slavery, and thus a complete violation of the respect owed workers qua humans.[1] A more modest but still powerful argument is based on the simple idea that workers, as humans, are born "free and equal in dignity and rights." From such starting points, the intrinsic justifications for democratizing work are analogous to justifications for democracy in other realms: the same way that there should be "no representation without taxation," as was demanded in the American Revolution, there should be no production—of goods or of services—without some form of representation in decisions relating to the organization within which that production occurs. The only meaningful form of respect for workers in the workplace is to grant them a meaningful voice about all relevant firm decisions.

The second set of reasons for democratizing work is instrumental. As with the intrinsic justification for democratizing work, the core of the instrumental justification is simple: democracy would increase an organization's collective intelligence, which would help it make better decisions, including more just ones. Because a democratized organization would have access to a greater diversity of information, points of view, and skill sets at all levels, particularly at the top, its capability for making good decisions would be strengthened considerably, likely balancing any potential cost in conflict and time. Furthermore, workers in a democratized organization would feel that their responsibilities had a bigger scope than merely protecting their jobs, meaning they would be more likely to put forth the information and effort required to make good decisions in the democratic process.[2]

It is only logical to assume that better decisions would translate to better economic performance. We already know that cooperatives, which are run by employee representatives, are not less competitive economically than nondemocratic organizations. Some

---

1. David Ellerman, *Property and Contract in Economics: The Case for Economic Democracy* (Cambridge, MA: Basil Blackwell, 1992).

2. What is true for an organization plausibly holds true for individual relations between employers and employees as well. A gardener or a cleaner whose human autonomy is respected by their employer is more likely to provide higher-quality labor than one submitted to strict orders and constant micro-management that deprives them of initiative and voice in matters that concerns them.

research shows that they may actually be more competitive.[3] The connection between democracy's better decisions and organizational performance becomes even clearer if we widen our definition of performance beyond mere economic indicators—especially if we include worker satisfaction as one of those performance indicators. Improved worker satisfaction in turn drives success in other areas since it has a strong positive influence on the resilience of both organizations and work relationships.

Democratizing work would have many other positive effects. The first of these is *less wage inequality and less distributive injustice in firms*. In nondemocratic companies in the United States, the average wage ratio of top earners in a company to those at the middle of the pay scale is 1 to 281 (as of 2017). In other words, the CEO of an average American company makes 281 times more than a typical employee.

In a democratized firm, this ratio would shrink. Indecently high salaries (Elon Musk, for example, made $595 million in 2019!) would be scaled down, while indecently low ones would scale up. In the Mondragon cooperative in Spain, the ratio of the lowest to the highest salary is 1 to 6. Minimum wage at Costco, which functions as a consumer cooperative responsive to its member base along democratic lines, is $20. By contrast, minimum wage at Walmart, the United States's leading retail corporation, is $11.50.

Even in times of crisis, as salaries and bonuses for most employees are kept stagnant or cut at every possible opportunity, boards and executives have arranged to be paid massive salaries and to be let go with golden parachutes—rewards that have no real connection to their actual contributions to company performance. More democratically governed organizations would likely render the current behaviors of boards and executives obsolete: these kinds of decisions would be impossible to justify to representatives of all employees.

The second advantage to democratized workplaces would be *less domination and discrimination*.

Democratizing work, which means in part making management more answerable to workers, would indeed shrink the possibility of domination in the workplace. It would make it possible to better

---

3. Fathi Fakhfakh, Virginie Pérotin, and Monica Gago, "Productivity, Capital, and Labor in Labor-Managed and Conventional Firms: An Investigation on French Data," *Industrial and Labor Relations Review* 65, no. 4 (2012): 847–879.

attend to workplace discrimination against women and minorities. We know this from history. Cooperatives organized by the American Black community in the aftermath of the Civil War as a response to discrimination in and outside their (white) places of work made economic and moral survival of Black workers possible through even the worst moments of American history, including the terrors of the Jim Crow era and the Great Depression of the 1930s.[4] We can also predict the beneficial effects of workers representation at the top of firm hierarchies. Women, racialized communities, and people with disabilities are extremely underrepresented in management positions and in boards of directors and overrepresented at the bottom, where they are more exposed to discrimination and abuses of power and therefore more likely to be aware of them. Democratizing work would provide new opportunities to ensure that problems of this type are taken up at the highest levels of power, by people similar to them, with similar experiences in the workplace. This would be even more likely if democratic representatives were chosen by lottery[5] rather than through the election of candidates, which tends to reproduce hegemony of all varieties.

A third benefit of democratized workplaces would be *social justice and resilience in the management of economic crises*. Negotiations are different in democratic organizations, and this stands out most starkly in periods of difficulty. During the 2008 financial crisis, the Mondragon cooperative had to close Fagor, one of its consumer goods factories. Before it came to this decision, however, its democratic government structure sought a variety of other solutions: first it redistributed work hours and lowered salaries across the board to keep on the greatest possible number of employees. When it became clear that the economic decision to close was unavoidable, the cooperative provided support to everyone who had been laid off, guaranteeing them jobs in its other companies and continuing to pay significant unemployment benefits until they had found new employment.

4. Jessica Gordon Nembhard, *Collective Courage: A History of African American Cooperative Economic Thought and Practice* (University Park, PA: Pennsylvania State University Press, 2014).

5. I argue for this form of open democracy in Hélène Landemore, *Open Democracy: Reinventing Popular Rule for the 21st Century* (Princeton, NJ: Princeton University Press, 2020).

A fourth positive outcome of democratizing workplaces would be *its impact on the environment and public health*. It is striking to note that in most recent cases where business leaders have taken climate change into account in their decisions, they have done so in response to pressure from employees, activists, and outside public opinion— not from shareholders.[6] Just as democratic organizations deal better and more justly with crises, we may predict that democratic organizations would react differently to environmental issues. Consider the difference between the choices shareholder representatives and worker representatives would likely make if confronted with the following dilemma: adopt a new and polluting technology that increases profits or forgo it to preserve the environment and the health of people living in the area. Shareholders and their representatives do not live near factory sites: they have the means to live elsewhere, in places that are protected from the immediate consequences of their decisions. Workers, by contrast, who often live near the factories where they work and cannot afford to move easily, would think twice about using a technology that took a significant toll on the health and environment of themselves and their communities.

The final advantage to democratizing work is that *it strengthens democracy everywhere*. Giving voice to individuals in the organizations and relationships where they spend most of their time means giving them an opportunity to exercise the voice they are supposed to have, but are so rarely able to express, in the civic and public sphere. Many thinkers, including J. S. Mill, W. E. B. Du Bois, J. Dewey, and C. Pateman, have hypothesized that in order to thrive, active citizenship requires families, communities, and companies that foster and encourage the democratic values of participation and equality, and this has been corroborated by widely available empirical data. When workers engage in political activities in the context of cooperatives,

6. Somini Sengupta and Veronica Penney, "Big Tech Has a Big Climate Problem: Now, It's Being Forced to Clean Up," *New York Times*, July 21, 2020, sec. Climate. Accessed September 2021, https://www.nytimes.com/2020/07/21/climate/apple-emissions-pledge.html. See also actions undertaken in 2019 by Amazon and Google employees: Colin Lecher, "Thousands of Amazon Employees Ask the Company to Adopt a Climate Change Plan," *The Verge*, April 10, 2019. Accessed September 2021, https://www.theverge.com/2019/4/10/18304800/amazon-employees-open-letter-climate-change-plan; Ruth Porat, "Google Workers for Action on Climate," *Medium* (blog), May 6, 2020. Accessed September 2021, https://medium.com/@googworkersac/ruth-porat-497bbb841b52.

it hones their taste and talent for political life outside of work. Workers who are accustomed to transparency and responsibility in the workplace will support these values in the public sphere as well.

Democratizing work is not a cure-all. The issue of workers in the gig economy and the informal economy ought to be the subject of its own set of reflections and accompanying measures. But democratizing work would nonetheless represent a substantial improvement in the everyday lives of hundreds of millions of workers all over the planet.

So How Do We Do It?

The first step toward democratizing work is, you might say, a question of vocabulary, of the way we use and define words. First among these words is *political,* whose core meaning we need to recover: it describes any organization or human relationship in which power relations exist—most crucially, for the topic of this book, the word *political* describes work and the workplace. It is time that we recognized the political nature of our places of work, such as companies, universities, and hospitals. They are *political entities,*[7] and they are currently being run by what the philosopher Elizabeth Anderson calls "private governments."[8] These private governments are not democracies. Most often, they take the form of restricted oligarchies, which, in very plain terms, means that control over the lives and futures of workers in most workplaces is restricted to people with money invested in them, called shareholders.

Democratizing the "private governments" of these firms means giving voice to anyone who contributes to them through what Isabelle Ferreras has called a "labor investment." This includes anyone who participates directly in the production of goods or services as well as individuals who contribute in less palpable ways to the human community that drives a firm—most importantly, those providing care to others. Contributors to the firm's human community are an expansive category and might include customers, users, or subcontracted workers.

7. Isabelle Ferreras, *Firms as Political Entities: Saving Democracy through Economic Bicameralism* (Cambridge: Cambridge University Press, 2017).

8. Elizabeth Anderson, *Private Government* (Princeton, NJ: Princeton University Press, 2017).

In concrete terms, democratizing work means vesting workers with decision-making power, including at the highest levels—in other words, opening company boards to them. Until now, workers have been shut out at this level, with some minimal exceptions in Germany, the Netherlands, the Scandinavian countries, and a handful of other European countries,[9] as well as, of course, a minority of producer cooperatives across the world.

To democratize, firms and other similar organizations would have to create institutional structures that make it possible for power to be shared with workers or their legitimate representatives. (Representation could be rethought as well: elections might be held, as they are for shareholder representatives on most boards today, or new methods of selection could be used, such as lotteries.) To foster the growth of firm democracy, governments could offer tax incentives for the creation of cooperatives and for the creation or conversion of companies with legal structures that institutionalize democratic principles of power sharing.

In the final analysis, the most compelling and urgent reason to democratize work is that it strengthens political democracy. In a time when democracies are under threat, the democratization of work may help foster a virtuous cycle that could help pass laws and policies (for example, a universal basic income or job guarantee) or ratify international agreements and treaties to secure the rights of all workers, including the most vulnerable.

9. See, for example, the timid steps France has taken in this direction with its 2019 PACTE Law, which requires that two or three worker representatives be elected to the governing boards of very large firms.

"As we face the monstrous risk of the pandemic and environmental collapse, making these strategic changes would allow us to ensure the dignity of all citizens while marshalling the collective strength and effort we need to preserve our life together on this planet."

EQUAL DIGNITY FOR ALL CITIZENS MEANS EQUAL VOICE AT WORK

The Importance of Epistemic Justice

LISA HERZOG

As Hélène Landemore has said, one of the most important benefits—and goals—of democratizing work is to strengthen democracy in our societies as a whole. A democratic society is one in which all individuals have equal dignity and an equal voice, where one's voice can be heard by others and will not be silenced without good reason. This basic principle has often been applied to the political realm, but if it is to organize our societies, it must also be applied in the world of work. It is difficult to find a workplace that is structured by this principle, however: most of our work lives are characterized by more or less livable situations of unequal power and one-sided dependence. Even when workers are not overtly commanded to keep quiet, the implicit fear of losing one's job or being penalized in other ways leads individuals to silence themselves. This means that many people, especially those who live and work at the margins of our societies, end up not only invisible but inaudible as well. Our societies cannot hope to be truly democratic if its members spend the bulk of their waking lives working in situations that ignore their right to equal dignity and equal voice.

In philosophy, there is a term for the kind of silencing I am talking about: it is called *epistemic injustice*.[1] It can range from not being taken seriously as an equal partner in conversation to not even having the words to describe one's experiences. This form of injustice exists because of social hierarchies based on gender, race, age, or socioeconomic status. It may be objected that epistemic injustice is less important than all the other material and symbolic injustices suffered by disadvantaged groups, including disenfranchised workers, in our economic systems. But epistemic injustice is inextricably intertwined with other forms of injustice, and it intensifies them by robbing people of the force of their voices and preventing them from speaking up. When a person speaks up about injustices, others with similar experiences can join forces with them: many social movements have begun with people telling their own stories. Indeed, listening to one another's voices and becoming aware of one another's stories is a precondition for joint political action. Epistemic injustice can nip that action in the bud. Speaking up is meaningless if one has no hope of being listened to or if one lacks the terms and concepts necessary to make one's perspective understood. Those who have no voice cannot fight for their own interests, material or symbolic, leaving it to other, more privileged individuals to decide whether or not they might want to speak for them, amplifying epistemic injustice and thus reinforcing other forms of material and symbolic injustice.[2] If our democratic societies are to thrive, we must fortify the capability of each of their members to express their voice.

The workplace is one place we should begin: as I have said, most workers experience some form of silencing in the workplace, and if they are nonmale, nonwhite, or from disadvantaged socioeconomic backgrounds, this silencing intersects with and reinforces other forms of injustice. To be sure, there are pragmatic limitations on how

---

1. It was coined by Miranda Fricker, *Epistemic Injustice: Power and the Ethics of Knowing* (Oxford: Oxford University Press, 2007). The adjective *epistemic* refers to the quality of knowledge and understanding and the capability to make oneself understood that comes with it.

2. *Yes, I am well aware that as an academic I am arguing for epistemic justice from a somewhat paradoxical position. In an epistemically just world, others would speak for themselves, and we academics would speak much less. But in the world we live in, we have the privilege of being able to make ourselves heard, of having access to newspapers and publishing houses. We want to use this privilege to speak up for reforms that would enable others to speak for themselves. And we want to continue the dialogue with them, to listen to them, and to learn from them.*

many people can speak at a time, meaning it may be necessary to elect spokespeople; there may be differential forms of expertise that justify differential epistemic authority on specific subject matters—but all too often these are trotted out as justifications for not acknowledging that all people should still have a *say*. Democratic practices in the workplace must allow individuals' voices to be expressed. Anything less constitutes an assault on their equal dignity.

All too often, however, questions of pragmatism and efficiency are used as justifications for maintaining sexist or racist prejudices about who "has something to say," reinforcing epistemic injustice. These justifications are often used with regard to groups at the margin of the so-called labor market: informal workers, or those who are formally independent contractors, all of whom are at greater risk of being silenced as sexualized or racialized minorities as well. One important step that could be taken to combat epistemic injustice would be to legally recognize the rights of such workers to a collective and individual voice in the processes of organizing work. Unions and political parties need to include the rights of these workers in their agendas. In Western countries in particular, this means addressing working conditions in the supply chain and among subcontractors. Just as the right to voice cannot end at the boundaries of a gender or a racial identity, it cannot end at national borders or only apply to those with a certain passport.

Epistemic justice is a matter of equal dignity, but that is not all. It has a pragmatic dimension too: as Hélène Landemore mentions in her essay, democracies in which all citizens have an equal voice can harness the power of the "knowledge of the many," which improves decision-making and helps errors be detected early on. A democratic society is a "learning" society: it has access to more knowledge and more perspectives and to the lessons of many more mistakes. Epistemic justice in workplaces, brought about by respecting the voices, rights, and interests of their employees and of their stakeholders, would help them become "learning organizations"—not for the sake of higher profits but for the sake of fulfilling meaningful roles in society at a time when society needs them most.[3]

---

3. See also Lisa Herzog and Felix Gerlsbeck, "The Epistemic Potentials of Workplace Democracy," *Review of Social Economy* 78, no. 3 (2020): 307–330.

Our societies face numerous tremendous challenges that must be addressed urgently. Climate change and environmental remediation, which are explicitly mentioned in the Manifesto, are among the most pressing, and they cannot be separated from other critical battles, against poverty, social injustice, and discrimination. In and out of the workplace, our societies must be learning societies in which knowledge is shared widely and by many. For this to happen, individuals need to be able to encounter one another as equals, to exchange arguments and ideas: we need epistemic justice, in other words.

The hierarchies that are common in the work world are deeply inimical to the learning processes necessary for an organization to become a learning organization. Unequal power distorts communications, fostering a climate in which "the boss only gets the good news." If knowledge is power, and workers are disempowered, then it is only to be expected that workers will use knowledge strategically to protect their interests, rather than communicating it freely. Problems at the bottom of an unequal hierarchy cause problems at the top: those with disproportionate power suffer epistemically because they must rely on the reports of others, which, as we have seen, cannot be expected to be straightforwardly accurate. Leaders who care about the fate of their organizations need to make sure that they receive honest feedback within social structures in which mutual trust is possible—in other words, within social structures that provide workers a secure and equal right to voice. The democratizing work movement will, we hope, include company owners and managers who wish to foster learning within their organizations. By experimenting with different strategies of democratization and contributing to social learning processes in the realm of work, they can help show the broader public that other kinds of companies are possible, helping to shift the worldview of "there is no alternative"[4] and delegitimize models in which workers are treated as "mere resources."

The Manifesto's call for a job guarantee can also contribute to epistemic justice by shifting power relations at work. As we discussed at the beginning of this essay, individuals who do not have other job alternatives may not feel fully empowered to make use of their right to voice even in cases where they have one. Many privileged

4. Lisa Herzog, *Reclaiming the System: Moral Responsibility, Divided Labour, and the Role of Organizations in Society* (Oxford: Oxford University Press, 2018).

workers with skills and credentials that carry market value, aware they are able to find another job, do dare to speak up against abuses, injustices, or dysfunctionalities within their organizations, but less privileged workers often do not have this luxury. A well-designed job guarantee, as the Manifesto suggests, could give all workers reasonable alternatives to fall back on, thus emboldening them to use their voices. This could be a game changer with regard to power relations in workplaces and help remedy epistemic injustice in and outside of the workplace.

By democratizing and decommodifying work, workers are empowered to use their voices—voices we need to hear to find solutions to the many threats we currently face. Changes in the work world must go hand in hand with other efforts to empower those who have been disproportionally silenced due to categorizations of gender, race, and socioeconomic status. The Black Lives Matter movement, along with other, ongoing struggles to achieve justice for nonmale individuals of all backgrounds, go hand in hand with struggles to improve workers' right to a voice. The most disadvantaged workers who suffer the greatest levels of epistemic injustice are often the most disadvantaged in other spheres of life as well.

Without changes in the world of work, epistemic injustice will persist. The question of whose voice is heard will continue to be answered by relations of power, with economic power chief among them. Democratic societies cannot continue to accept these distortions in their public discourse and in relations among their citizens, in private life and at work. The democratic promise of equal dignity cannot be kept unless we make an effort to bring about epistemic justice and ensure that all people are able to develop the capabilities and habits of speaking their minds—that all people have the chance to be heard.

"If we leave these things solely to the market, we run the risk of exacerbating inequalities to the point of forfeiting the very lives of the least advantaged."

DEMOCRATIZING WORK TO REVERSE INCREASING INEQUALITIES

IMGE KAYA-SABANCI

Moving from Lisa Herzog's discussion of the importance of correcting epistemic injustice and reinforcing the equal dignity of all voices by democratizing workplaces, I would like to open on a hopeful observation about voice: thousands of people have already mobilized and engaged with the democratizing work manifesto, and beyond that, around the world, people are ready to shoulder responsibility, take action, and change our current dysfunctional practices for the sake of a better future. They *want* to be heard and recognized as equals, even as the pandemic has deepened existing inequalities and magnified their devastating consequences.

Overall, the most undervalued and underserved sectors of society—women, members of racialized communities, migrants, the working poor—have suffered the worst in the coronavirus crisis. In this essay, I will focus on one of the largest groups suffering from inequalities: women. Today, not a single country has achieved gender equality, and according to the latest *Global Gender Gap Report*, gender parity will not be achieved for 135.6 more years. Women and girls are consistently undervalued; they cannot access equal opportunities; they often work more and usually earn less. Furthermore, they suffer from multiple forms of violence, both at home and in public spaces.

And that was *before* the pandemic struck. The COVID-19 crisis worsened this already outrageous and unequal situation in myriad ways. Violence against women increased tremendously: France, for example, reported a 32 percent increase in domestic violence in just one week of the lockdown period, and the United Nations estimates similar explosive increases across the globe. Women have suffered professionally as well: in academia for instance, the productivity of female scholars has dropped much more steeply than that of their male peers.[1]

These sad developments are directly related to the ways in which we conceptualize work as a commodity, which engenders job precariousness, particularly in jobs predominantly held by women. Social distancing measures have led to greater unemployment in industries where women make up a majority of workers, such as care, hospitality, and education.[2] Moreover, jobs in the informal economy and low-wage jobs in general, where women also make up the bulk of the workforce, have been the hardest hit by the economic crisis. In the field of entrepreneurship, my area of expertise, female entrepreneurs, in addition to the barriers they faced before the crisis, are now less likely to gain to access crisis support mechanisms.

The gendered ways our societies conceptualize domestic work further complicate the social and economic problems faced by women.[3] School and daycare center closures have added to the workload of unpaid care. UNESCO has estimated the percentage of students affected by school closures worldwide at more than 91 percent, or nearly 1.6 billion children. Considering the current distribution of care duties, it is evident that this situation has affected women more unfavorably than men. These problems are even more intense for single mothers, who make up the majority of single-parent households (e.g., 85 percent in the EU). These increased care responsibilities leave women less time and energy to focus on their work. Taken together, these facts are proof of the disproportionate negative

---

1. David Matthews, "Pandemic Lockdown Holding Back Female Academics, Data Show," *Times Higher Education*, June 25, 2020.

2. Titan Alon, Matthias Doepke, Jane Olmstead-Rumsey, and Michèle Tertilt, "The Impact of COVID-19 on Gender Equality," no. w26947, National Bureau of Economic Research, 2020.

3. Cecilia L. Ridgeway, *Framed by Gender: How Gender Inequality Persists in the Modern World* (Oxford: Oxford University Press, 2011).

effects of the crisis on women, who now face more violence, deepened poverty, greater risk of unemployment, and extra housework. In sum, inequality has been exacerbated.

Inequalities based on income, sex, age, disability, sexual orientation, race, class, ethnicity, religion, and opportunity are not only negative for the groups they affect directly. They also harm society as a whole. They affect all dimensions of life, including social and human development, health, education, and civic life,[4] as well as future economic growth and stability.[5] They demolish people's sense of fulfillment and self-worth. This, in turn, can lead to crime, disease, and environmental degradation.[6] By contrast, increasing equalities is a cornerstone and a prerequisite for communities and economies to thrive and for the planet to be safe and protected. An equal world is also a healthier, happier, and more prosperous one.

My work experience with underserved women, not only from my home country, Turkey, but also from the Middle East, Africa, and South Asia, has given me firsthand experience with contentious sociopolitical contexts, where certain sectors of society are systematically underserved, discriminated against, and silenced. My experiences in these regions, supported by research, have shown me that rising authoritarianism and weakening democracies go hand in hand with the underrepresentation of women in decision-making mechanisms and lead to an increase in gender inequality. Moreover, it has been observed that antidemocratic practices at the top can easily diffuse to microspaces. It is heartening to see that the antidemocratic endeavors of authoritarian administrations are being met with backlash from the public, which is enthusiastically demanding more democracy and more inclusive models of governance all over the world.

But how can we reduce inequalities and ensure that no one is left behind? Equality can only be achieved and sustained through democratic principles. Certainly, it is crucial to strengthen the functioning of democratic practices in the political arena, but democratizing

4. Hari Bapuji, Charmi Patel, Gokhan Ertug, and David G. Allen, "Corona Crisis and Inequality: Why Management Research Needs a Societal Turn," *Journal of Management* 46, no. 7 (September 2020): 1205–1222.

5. Facundo Alvaredo, Lucas Chancel, Thomas Piketty, Emmanuel Saez, and Gabriel Zucman, eds., *World Inequality Report 2018* (Cambridge, MA: Belknap Press, 2018).

6. United Nations, *Equality: Why It Matters* (2017).

central legislative and executive branches alone will not suffice to lessen or eradicate inequalities. We also need to build social change, to demand more democracy from the bottom up. To this end, we must democratize firms to ensure that workers are represented in firm governance and decisions regarding their lives. We need to give voice to the people who are the core constituency of firms so that firms do not contribute to and reproduce existing inequalities.

Sustainable development and a more prosperous life on this planet can only be achieved if all people have access to equal rights and are not excluded from opportunities and decision-making processes affecting their own lives. Democracy is based on this same principle, that all people are equal and that everyone ought to have an equal voice in deciding the direction of policies. If democracy is central to the well-being of our societies, why are firms, which are the main engines of our economies and deeply embedded in social life, still exempt from applying basic democratic principles to their governance? This manifesto on democratizing work highlights the deep connection between antidemocratic governance models and social and economic inequalities, including the ones I have described here.

We must take concrete steps to tackle inequality and the intricacies associated with it. The market, we have seen over and over, fails to ensure equal representation on its own. Our governments should not shy away from proactive measures. For instance, to address women's underrepresentation in decision-making positions, quotas that require a certain percentage of women on corporate boards are in place for publicly listed companies in several European countries. But until we have completely done away with the institutional and structural discrimination that leads to gender inequality and the underrepresentation of women, we should be brave enough to open up a public debate on establishing gender quotas with broader scope.

Many people are now aware we cannot continue as before. Antidemocratic practices have produced the world in which we find ourselves today, an unequal world where millions of people suffer, a planet that has lost countless species and where a million more are threatened with extinction, an Earth where our very existence is endangered by climate change and the natural disasters it causes. We cannot afford to lose more lives or to silence diverse voices anymore.

It is time to heed the crucial call of the democratizing work manifesto. Excluding some groups from decision-making mechanisms, muting certain sectors of society, and silencing life at large are all intrinsically connected. We cannot celebrate life unless we celebrate its many voices, with inclusive models of governance that effectively tackle inequalities, including the ones women face so painfully.

"The dignity of their jobs needs no other explanation than that eloquently simple term essential worker."

WORK IN DIGNITY

ADELLE BLACKETT

On March 18, 1968, only a few weeks before his assassination, the Rev. Dr. Martin Luther King Jr. lent his moral power to a movement of African American sanitation workers in Memphis, Tennessee. They were striking for union recognition and economic justice. In the face of their deplorable, segregated working conditions, which cost many of them their lives at work, their cry was one of basic human dignity: "I am a man." King said to them:

> So often we overlook the work and the significance of those who are not in professional jobs, of those who are not in the so-called big jobs. But let me say to you tonight, that whenever you are engaged in work that serves humanity and is for the building of humanity, it has dignity, and it has worth. One day our society must come to see this. One day our society will come to respect the sanitation worker if it is to survive, for the person who picks up our garbage, in the final analysis, is as significant as the physician, for if he doesn't do his job, diseases are rampant. All labor has dignity.[1]

1. Rev. Dr. Martin Luther King Jr., *All Labor Has Dignity* (Boston, MA: Beacon Press, 1963/2011): 172.

Dr. King's words ring out with unmistakable clarity and renewed urgency in the COVID-19 pandemic. For over a year now, society has rapidly been forced to accept that "the person who picks up our garbage [. . .] is as significant as the physician"—and so are the grocery store workers, hospital orderlies, and agricultural workers. Much has changed since Dr. King spoke to that assembly of sanitation workers, but the pandemic has shone a spotlight on the depth of persisting disparities, including the extent to which essential workers' own needs remain "invisible." Many are racialized, low-wage workers with irregular migration status. Most lack the social protection necessary to care for their families in dignity. Globally, the magnitude of the informal economy and yawning inequality among and within states compounds this problem. Many countries fail—due to a variety of reasons, from political deadlock to lack of resources—to roll out the kind of social protection measures that would enable workers to protect themselves and their families.

Dr. King launched his Poor Peoples' Campaign to combat the injustice of racialized economic disadvantage, but its goal was to underscore the common cause of *all* the disinherited women and men of this earth. The campaign was deeply rooted both in an understanding of wealthy nations' responsibility to act and in a commitment to a profound internationalism that made common cause with the peoples of the Global South. Dr. King faced tremendous backlash from a comfortable liberal establishment: he may be remembered as a "nonviolent dreamer," but the depth of the critique this "inconvenient hero"[2] faced for a philosophy that challenged racism, materialism, and militarization reveals the magnitude of the break he sought from the prevailing status quo. Dr. King was particularly troubled by critiques from this quarter—from those who out of fear, or out of indifference, stood in the way of justice by clinging to the way things were.

Today's movements to democratize, decommodify, and decarbonize must follow King's example and engage with the ways in which calls for action on behalf of workers at society's margins challenge a status quo that is comfortable for a few and profoundly inequitable for many others. The #DemocratizingWork manifesto

2. Vincent Harding, *Martin Luther King: The Inconvenient Hero* (Maryknoll, NY: Orbis Books, 1996/2008).

challenges particular forms of hardened global regulation that have served to "prevent state projects of egalitarian redistribution,"[3] leading to soaring inequality. The initiative embodies growing acknowledgment of the need to reclaim policy space for social regulation, pushing back against the fictitious commodification of both labor and land.[4] The Manifesto draws attention to workers—of the South and of the North—"who are not in the so-called big jobs," urging us not only to truly *see* them but also to work to change the terms under which they perform their labor. Then, as now, the cry is one of basic human dignity: essential workers are not simply there to risk their lives "serving" those of us able to quarantine. They are women. They are men. They are human.

When I signed the #DemocratizingWork statement in solidarity, I reached out to the authors to urge an acknowledgment of racialization, migration, and informality. The authors responded to my solidarity in kind. Together, we say: so much more *essential* work is necessary to grapple with white supremacy, the "unnamed political system that has made the modern world what it is today."[5] Cedric Robinson has explained how racial capitalism is a broad notion with a long history, including in Europe.[6] It helps us understand the centuries-long transatlantic slave trade as a global institution and acknowledge that capitalism continues to advance on divided terrain.[7] Incessant anti-Black racism and murderous brutality constitute a pandemic within the pandemic, and the need to place Black lives at the center of our attention is urgently necessary. After the world witnessed the horrific eight-minute-forty-six-second video at the heart of #JusticeforGeorgeFloyd, which Pulitzer Prize winner Darnella Frazier had the courage to take and share, the urgency is also finally being broadly acknowledged. #DemocratizingWork has a crucial role to play by making a justice claim that encompasses the call for economic justice, racial equality, and work in dignity.

3. Quinn Slobodian, *Globalists: The End of Empire and the Birth of Neoliberalism* (Cambridge, MA: Harvard University Press, 2018).
4. Karl Polanyi, *The Great Transformation* (Boston, MA: Beacon Press, 1944/2001).
5. Charles W. Mills, *The Racial Contract* (Ithaca, NY: Cornell University Press, 1997).
6. Cedric Robinson, *Black Marxism: The Making of the Black Radical Tradition* (Chapel Hill, NC: University of North Carolina Press, 2000).
7. Stuart Hall, *The Fateful Triangle* (Cambridge, MA: Harvard, 2017).

With the legacy of Dr. King and the striking sanitation workers in mind, and as Hélène Landemore and Lisa Herzog recall in this volume, going forward a core concern must be *human dignity* at work. Although some of the policy recommendations of the Manifesto have their roots in Europe and a state-centered worldview, the multilevel character of #DemocratizingWork can and should transcend these specificities. States matter, but so, too, does action transnationally, including at the regional and international levels. The Manifesto's transnational call for guaranteed employment draws on the terms of Article 23 of the Universal Declaration of Human Rights, which affirms that *everyone* has the "right to work, to free choice of employment, to just and favourable conditions of work and to protection against unemployment" and that "everyone, without any discrimination, has the right to equal pay for equal work." Article 23 refocuses attention on the right for "everyone who works" to enjoy "just and favourable remuneration," ensuring the worker and their family "an existence worthy of human dignity, and supplemented, if necessary, by other means of social protection." Moreover, Article 23 concludes that "everyone has the right to form and to join trade unions for the protection of his interests." Consider the striking sanitation workers' demands in this light. Moving forward to the present, consider that most workers worldwide are part of a complex, amorphous informal economy, which presses down on them with the weight of history: of colonialism, of unfreedom. This informal economy epitomizes a yawning inequality that calls us to question current paradigms for the governance of labor. Many of COVID-19's essential workers are also precarious workers, and too often they fall outside of labor law's traditional boundaries. Truly acknowledging the equal dignity of all workers requires nothing less than a fundamental rethink of the idea of labor law. We must recenter redistributive goals beyond borders. We must, in other words, decolonize.

The constitution of the International Labour Organization (ILO) affirms that labor is not a commodity. It asks that we "examine and consider all international economic and financial policies and measures" in light of their capacity to foster social justice. When accepting the Nobel Peace Prize in 1969, representatives of the ILO acknowledged that the organization needed to question industrial development models it had inadvertently sought to universalize throughout the Global South. The ILO's 2012 Social Protection

Floors Recommendation (No. 202) holds potential to offer particular insight for rethinking the living conditions that put precarious workers—including domestic workers and migrant agricultural workers—at particular risk of COVID-19.[8] Thinking on job guarantees, decent working conditions, and social protection must embody North-South and South-South solidarity; it must include regions in the process of rethinking the spaces for distributive justice.[9] Reclaiming regulatory capacity in the various spaces where economic governance is operated to craft social justice alternatives is as much an act of legal imagination as it is a tremendous policy challenge. It requires us to be deliberate in acknowledging the weight of history on relationships with the Global South and the South of the North and to make it a priority to decolonize labor law.

Particularly in the past months, I have wondered how many people think of domestic workers when they think of the Montgomery, Alabama bus boycotts at the height of the US civil rights movement led by Dr. King. Domestic workers were at the forefront of their movement, walking to work in massive numbers to support the boycott and acting at great cost to claim their rights.[10] It is a powerful reminder that workers must lead their own movements if those movements are to be effective. Academics, too, have a pivotal role to play—by listening deeply, by framing, by bringing the fruit of our research in support of societal transformation. The global fund for universal social protection championed by the International Trade Union Confederation is an important example of how academics may contribute to worker-led movements as the COVID-19 pandemic lingers. #DemocratizingWork holds the potential to be an emancipatory movement if its members have the strength to accept, as did Dr. King, that we all must live with and work through critique, discomfort, and even backlash as we walk together on the road to social justice and dignity for all.

---

8. Adelle Blackett, *Everyday Transgressions: Domestic Workers' Transnational Challenge to International Labor Law* (Ithaca, NY: Cornell University Press, 2019).

9. Adelle Blackett, "Theorizing Emancipatory Transnational Futures of International Labour Law" *American Journal of International Law Unbound* 113 (2020): 390; Adelle Blackett, "On Social Regionalism in Transnational Labour Law," *International Labour Review* 159, no. 4 (2020): 591–613.

10. Premilla Nadasen, *Household Workers Unite: The Untold Story of African American Women Who Built a Movement* (Boston, MA: Beacon Press, 2015).

"A personal investment of labor, that is, of one's mind and body, one's health—one's very life—ought to come with the collective right to validate or veto [. . .] decisions."

DUAL MAJORITIES FOR FIRM GOVERNMENTS

SARA LAFUENTE

After decades of global neoliberal financial capitalism, institutions of industrial democracy face a singular set of challenges: erosion, decentralization, fragmentation, competition, weakened unions, and more. In her essay, Adelle Blackett points out how some of the very ways we think about labor law (and react to worker movements and demands) cannot account for or hope to correct the unequal reality of a colonized, racialized world, a topic Flávia Máximo expands on as well. In our fragmented context, issuing a call to democratize work may seem daunting in the sense that it cannot mean the same thing in all places nor to all people.[1] To me, though, democratizing work is a transformative, integrative, and transnational project. Of course, my standpoint is rooted in Europe's systems of industrial relations, but, by exploring the positive aspects and the weaknesses of these systems, I would like to point to ways in which industrial relations *can* reinforce the collective power of workers—starting from within firms. In the context of global capitalism, this would mean giving real power to workers in firms and in the economy by

1. Stan De Spiegelaere et al., "Democracy at Work," in *Benchmarking Working Europe*, ETUI and ETUC (Brussels: ETUI, 2019): 67–89.

granting them the concrete means to exercise a collective voice in decision-making, under the aegis of broadly articulated regulations, framed transnationally.

Today, this is hardly the case: in works councils and codetermined boards of directors alike, labor representatives sense that they have restricted and insufficient access to the information and expertise they need. Decisions are, for the most part, made "elsewhere," and worker input rarely leads to changing them substantively. With no true parity and no collective veto rights, workers cannot enter negotiations on an equal footing with their employers, who continue to represent the interests of those who contribute capital to firms.

In that sense, even the most favorable existing forms of codetermination represent a combination of promise and disappointment: under the "false" parity of German codetermination (*Mitbestimmung*), workers never enjoy a real majority in supervisory boards. While half of the members of these boards are worker representatives and the other half represent capital, the board's president is always a representative of capital, who casts the deciding vote in case of a tie. Under "strict" parity codetermination (*Montan-Mitbestimmung*), which applies only to a few German companies operating in the metal, coal, and steel industries—known as *Montan* industries—labor and shareholders have an equal number of seats on the supervisory board and jointly choose a "neutral" president. But even in these companies, votes are still made individually, toward a simple majority, as these supervisory boards are single bodies where votes representing capital and labor are not kept distinct. Decisions can thus be made against the will of the majority of labor representatives in cases where a single one of them votes with the shareholder representatives.[2] This kind of representative system structurally prevents worker interests from enjoying the benefits of truly collective representation in the board.

In Europe, firms enjoy freedom of enterprise, of establishment, and the free movement of capital. This allows them to circumvent the requirements to comply with workers' democratic rights in countries where these are recognized. Firms can avoid minimal requirements

---

2. Except to approve the appointment of the "director of labor relations," which requires a majority of favorable votes from labor representatives within the supervisory board.

for democratic representation in force in a given country by shifting their legal status, their size, or simply by picking up and moving their head offices to countries whose governments are less mindful of labor rights, particularly ones that do not require codetermination.

To a certain degree, transnational industrial relations do now exist and could counter this "regime shopping" effect across countries, but they remain limited. In Europe, multiemployer social dialogue is in crisis[3] and rarely succeeds in establishing reciprocal and binding obligations with regard to working conditions.[4] Admittedly, multinationals with more than one thousand employees and at least 150 employees in each of at least two member states are required to establish a European works council, a representative employee body that must be informed and consulted regarding certain types of decisions within a company. In a few companies, these councils have been made symbolically global. While these councils have the potential to be vehicles for collective representation and coordination, their rights are currently restricted, as they have no right to negotiate or to veto company strategy. All too often, they become battlegrounds for unequally represented national interests or, worse, end up as parodies of real deliberative spaces, serving only to lend a veneer of legitimacy to managerial decisions. Occasionally, their activity leads to the signing of ambiguous international framework agreements with timid content, which, despite union efforts at procedural clarification, are signed outside the bounds of any kind of normative framework. As for transnational board-level representation rights, the *Erzberger v. TUI AG* case C-566/15 throws sharp light on the limitations, or really the absence, of a European framework: in it, the European Court of Justice ruled that national codetermination laws can, without breaching EU law, exclude employees of foreign subsidiaries from choosing labor representatives to sit on the supervisory board of the group's parent company. We should neither ignore the existence of

3. The rulings handed down in the *EPSU v. European Commission* case, on the right of public servants to information and consultation within central governments, are recent evidence of this.

4. Christophe Degryse, *European Sectoral Social Dialogue: An Uneven Record of Achievement?* (Brussels: ETUI, 2015). Although, in contrast with the 2008 crisis, the pandemic has seemingly relaunched sectoral social dialogue at EU level. See Christophe Degryse, *'Union sacrée?' Les partenaires sociaux sectoriels face à la crise du Covid-19 en Europe* (Brussels: ETUI, 2021).

these institutional structures and their potential nor the improvements they demand.

With all this in mind, the Manifesto puts forward the possibility of introducing the radically democratic principle of *bicameralism*[5] into firm government. Bicameralism represents the structural recognition of conflicting interests, in which both capital and labor have their own representative bodies, adapted to their own specific organizational logic. It is a principle of government that would function in favor of *all* those who work in firms, giving them effective voice in the operational and strategic decisions made there. The basic idea of bicameralism is to expand the competencies of works councils as they exist today, giving them collective veto rights over strategic decisions and, in this way, evening the balance of power, which currently is heavily weighted in favor of capital. In addition to the symbolic value of officially recognizing the equal dignity and voice of workers within firms, bicameral firm government would have meaningful impact on the vote. To pass, a decision about firm policy made under this system would require majority approval *both* from shareholder representatives *and* from worker representatives. This is the radical difference between bicameralism and the systems of codetermination currently in place, including the German one: although they may recognize worker *votes*, they do not recognize workers' *collective voice* on the board. This exposes worker representatives to constraint and defensive bargaining, meaning they are at greater risk of being coopted, pressured, or simply finding it easier to go along with the projects of capital.

Of course, the question of reach or scope of application must be raised. In the current crisis, public aid to businesses comes with an opportunity to require companies receiving benefits to implement internal democracy, and national governments should seize this opportunity. In Spain, Portugal, Greece, and Ireland, this could be an occasion to revive agreements and laws that recognize workers' right to representation in state-owned companies, which have been demolished over the past decades with waves of privatization and weakening unions.

5. See the work of Isabelle Ferreras, *Gouverner le capitalisme? Pour le bicamérisme économique* (Paris : Presses universitaires de France, 2012) and *Firms as Political Entities: Saving Democracy through Economic Bicameralism* (Cambridge: Cambridge University Press, 2017).

But—and this is a big but—if we are to avoid commodification and ensure that democratic rights in the workplace are respected rather than flouted or ignored, the scope of action of such conditional aid, or, more broadly, of any initiative to democratize work, cannot be limited to the public sector, nor even to certain types of company—or to single nations.[6] To this end, the European Trade Union Confederation is demanding a European directive on minimum standards for the right to information, consultation, and worker representation on boards of directors, following an "escalator approach" with two or three employee representatives in companies with 50 to 250 employees, and one-third participation in companies with 250 to a thousand employees, until reaching parity in big companies with more than one thousand employees. This kind of directive has the potential for major impact if it is bold enough; namely, if its field of application could include all multinationals operating in Europe, and link labor representation in boards to veto rights for certain critical decisions. Finally, given the current crisis and the accompanying recession, requirements for democratization ought to be extended to bankruptcy, business recovery procedures, and worker buyouts. Experimentation with this in South America and in Europe deserves notice from union strategists and policy makers, with an eye to fostering buyouts under conditions that are favorable to workers organized in cooperatives or other collectives.[7]

The Manifesto has identified a concrete plan for structuring democracy within firms. However, the challenge of implementation remains: the reality of human and economic organization within today's firms transcends the legal contours of corporate law and national borders in ways that allow firms to slip the moorings of unions and industrial relations. Employers and management representatives are drifting further and further away from worker communities affected by their decisions; at the same time, worker communities are becoming more and more fragmented as employment status splinters, pushing workers across the globe into competition with

6. Aline Conchon, *Workers' Voice in Corporate Governance: A European Perspective* (Brussels: ETUI and ETUC, 2015).

7. Gemma Fajardo García, coord., *Empresas gestionadas por sus trabajadores. Problemática jurídica y social* (Valencia: CIRIEC, 2015). The transposition of EU 2019/1023 on preventive restructuring frameworks, discharge of debt, and insolvency is an opportunity for this.

one another, unchecked by any effective transnational regulatory framework. The possibility of solidarity among workers now often (and paradoxically) relies on the organizing capacity of the most powerful unions, who are less and less able to represent workers in the global economy as a whole.

Promoting democratic workplaces in a deregulated and undemocratic economy seems a difficult proposition, and it is clear that coordinating and interfacing with other collective labor institutions, particularly through sectoral collective bargaining and strong unions, is essential. Unions could embrace bicameralism in this context as a way to help repoliticize areas of the service economy where it is difficult to forge a strong union presence. It also presents an excellent opportunity to encourage affiliation and democratic initiatives beyond works council elections, as bicameralism would involve employee representatives in the workings of the firm. Nor would the strike lose any meaning or power, especially given its increasingly political usage mixed with other repertoires of action.[8]

This is the crux of the challenge: as we struggle to manage the COVID-19 crisis, it is necessary to create institutional conditions capable of helping to even the balance of power between capital and labor. The project of democracy in the workplace has sustained serious damage over the years. However, the current crisis opens up the possibility of a new social and political dynamic, breathing new life into the challenges and debates rippling through our societies. The success or failure of this new dynamic depends on whether and how much collective actors, particularly unions, are willing to take advantage of this opportunity. It also depends on their capacity to seize upon new and creative ideas, to mobilize, and to build alliances at the local and global levels to challenge dominant discourses while expanding interpretive frameworks and growing the scope of the possible.

---

8. Kurt Vandaele, "Interpreting Strike Activity in Western Europe in the Past 20 Years: the Labour Repertoire under Pressure," *Transfer* 22, no. 3 (2016): 277–294.

*"This crisis [. . .] shows that work must not be treated as a
commodity, that market mechanisms alone cannot be left in
charge of the choices that affect our communities most deeply."*

RESCUING JOURNALISM BY DECOMMODIFYING THE MEDIA

JULIA CAGÉ

Since one of the essential conditions of a functional democracy is a
free press, this essay will explain how journalism is damaged when
it is treated as a commodity and will discuss how democratizing
work can help save our news media. Each of us has emphasized the
ways in which *every* worker is first and foremost a citizen, capable
of participating in collective deliberations, both in companies and
in the civic arena, and here I am going to take a close look at how
this observation applies to the work world of journalists, touching
on how labor and corporate law should be revised to reflect this.

Pausing to speak out on behalf of journalists may seem surprising,
given our times, both because of the many other urgent problems
we face and because journalists are so mistrusted by a growing portion of the population. But for our democracies to function, all of
the branches of our system of checks and balances must be strong.
The weakening of the free press endangers the functioning of the
other branches. The media crisis the world is undergoing right now
is not confined to any one newspaper or website: what we are expe-
riencing is a crisis of commodification. Commodifying the work of
journalism restricts its freedom to inform and endangers freedom of
information in our societies. We are all affected by it, and it can only

be solved by democratizing the government and the shareholders of news media groups.

Declining trust in media has been caused in no small part by the erosion of editorial independence, which has been one result of successive rounds of recapitalization in the media world. These have helped save a certain number of news outlets over the past decades but often at the price of accepting investments from outside the media world. Although not all of these capital investments have brought any overt threat of censorship with them, the very presence of such investors raises at least two major concerns: first, self-censorship and, second, the disproportionate political clout that comes with owning a big name in news media. These threats intensify as ownership within the sector becomes increasingly concentrated.

The second cause of the current crisis in the media is linked to the overuse of one approach to the market. For decades, the news media employed an economic model that relied on a combination of sales and advertising revenue. The print media failed to see that these two revenue streams were headed toward inevitable collapse brought on by the introduction of new media that were more attractive to consumers and advertisers alike. This is not a new phenomenon: radio and television drove the first nails into the coffin of print media long ago. But the arrival of the internet—followed by the 2008 financial crisis and then by the coronavirus crisis—set off shockwaves on an entirely different scale. When the print news industry first observed that advertising revenue was drying up, it made the error of believing that the loss would be temporary. It turned a blind eye to the fact that as a percentage of GDP, advertising revenue for newspapers had been dropping since the 1950s. This failure to understand what was really going on was accompanied by a historic mistake for which we are still paying the price: newspapers decided to publish online editions for free on the assumption that advertising revenue would pay for them. They did not see what was truly at stake in this decision, which was the widespread devaluing of the news media. Over the long term, how would citizens understand the true costs of reporting the news when it was being delivered to them for free?

Newspapers gambled on online advertising revenue as part of a widespread embrace of an online advertising market. This, too, was a grave mistake: although certainly growing, the online advertising market rapidly came to be dominated by Big Tech and did not actually have much place for the news media. The upshot has been a never-ending race for the highest click-through rates and a proliferation of articles online, sometimes to the detriment of quality and often to the detriment of originality. More and more, copy-pasting and reposting has become the only viable strategy for online news media outlets that want to cover everything as quickly as possible, with an ever-shrinking workforce.[1] Online content has become extremely standardized as a result of this, obliterating any remaining idea of added value in the eyes of readers—an irony given that citizens actually place more value on original content now, due to careful reputation building over the long term and a preference for originality. Why have newspapers pursued this (re)production strategy? It is more profitable over the short term: in a world where the media—even the news—are commodities, rapid return on investment remains the driving measure of success.

This trend has been amplified by the increasing use of "native advertising," in which sponsored content is disguised as real content on the platform on which it appears, sacrificing reader trust for the sake of profit. From an economic perspective, native advertising lets newspapers fill their pages at no cost. Moreover, it has turned out to be extremely effective with readers, who are more easily swayed by it, making advertisers eager to pay for it. This is even truer online: native advertising is harder for ad-blocking software to identify, meaning that it garners more click-throughs.

To understand what is truly playing out with native advertising, it is helpful to look back at the history of the news media and recall the stock market dramas of the American press beginning in the 1960s. Newspaper operating margins grew then, not thanks to increased readership, but because of extreme austerity measures, of which workers were the primary victims, both through massive layoffs and the increasing use of freelancers. More recently, still-profitable media outlets have reacted to drops in advertising revenue by cutting jobs, voluntarily setting off a vicious cycle of profit seeking over quality: less advertising revenue, fewer journalists, lower quality, fewer readers, lower sales, less advertising revenue, fewer journalists, etc. Using native advertising is not the same as imposing austerity measures, of

1. Julia Cagé, Nicolas Hervé, and Marie-Luce Viaud, *L'information à tout prix* (Paris, Institut National de l'Audiovisuel, 2017).

course. But it does reflect the same trend of willingness among news media outlets to sacrifice their readers' trust (not to mention their employees) to raise profits *over the short term.* The current crisis in the media can only be solved by changing the very model under which news outlets operate. We must work together to create the conditions for independent media to thrive and prevent them from being governed by market forces alone. Journalists produce a public good: information. This public good cannot be produced by companies whose core objective is to maximize operating margins. Journalistic independence ought to be guaranteed through the creation of "nonprofit media companies,"[2] news companies whose only purpose is providing quality news—not satisfying the needs of their financial backers. Any profits earned by nonprofit media organizations would not be paid out as dividends to shareholders. Instead, they would be reinvested in operations. This could be done through different legal structures, such as a foundation or an association, their common design trait being that they would not be expected to produce financial profit for their shareholders.

Of course, the idea of decommodifying the work of journalism has received a certain amount of attention in recent years—why go further? Why not give news companies the legal status of foundation and have done with it? *This change alone is not enough.* In my opinion, *democratizing* the work of journalism is even more important and a goal we all too often tend to forget—if we are aware of it at all. The problem of decommodification without democratization is that merely turning all news outlets into nonprofits would not in any way address the issue of *power relations* in the media. We must ensure that media outlets are democratically governed in a way that includes staff and citizens. Whatever form nonprofit media organizations may take in the future, and bearing in mind that every aspect of a foundation depends on how its bylaws are written, who sits on its board, and what rules govern the mandates of board members, we must not restrict our focus to changing the ownership structure of our news organizations—we must democratize their governments as well.

---

2. This is the proposal I put forward in Julia Cagé, *Saving the Media: Capitalism, Crowdfunding and Democracy* (Cambridge, MA: Harvard University Press, 2016) [*Sauver les médias. Capitalisme, financement participatif et démocratie*, La République des Idées (Paris: Le Seuil, 2015)].

Democratic government in the media could take many forms. One alternative would be to design media government along the traditional lines of representative democracies using the principle of one person, one vote. Historically, there have been many cooperative news outlets designed around this model, but few have succeeded. Although it has served other sectors well, it does not seem to be the best choice of governance for the news media, where models based on the principle of one person, one voice lead, mathematically, to the dilution of journalists' political voice, since the latter are outnumbered by readers (one hopes, at least). After all, the ultimate goal of democratizing the news media is not only to win back ownership for those who consume it, but for those who produce it as well.

Alternatively, voting rights might be made separate from capital contributions by creating a participation threshold (for example, 10 percent of total capital investments) beyond which voting rights would not increase proportionally with capital contributions. In addition to such a threshold, it might also be stipulated that only a third of capital contributions come with extra voting rights; by the same token, those making smaller capital contributions might see their voting rights increase in inverse proportion. In cases where a news media company was structured as a nonprofit, it might be simpler to use a model inspired by corporations with different classes of shares, with a proportion of ordinary shares that come with one vote per share and another portion of special shares with weighted votes (generally ten per share). This kind of system was used when the *New York Times* went public and also, more recently, by Google. A media nonprofit might be structured with two categories of membership: "one-time" members, who make a single or very small contribution during a fundraising campaign, and "active" members, regular and committed donors who would have more seats on the nonprofit's board.

These two alternatives are based on existing institutional structures, but given the energy of creativity that has been poured into innovative new media in the past decade alone, there is no reason to stop there: as Sara Lafuente writes of the potential of bicameralism, once we have recognized the seeds of democracy in existing structures, we may begin to work toward new models that are transformative, integrative, and transnational to expand all citizens' rights to free access to information.

> *"A job guarantee would not only offer each person access to work that allows them to live with dignity, it would also provide a crucial boost to our collective capability to meet the many pressing social and environmental challenges we currently face."*

DECOMMODIFYING WORK

The Power of a Job Guarantee

PAVLINA R. TCHERNEVA

We work. We participate, care, and provide. We produce and re-produce. In the modern world, much of our work is commodified through private firms organizing production and employment for commercial return. Meanwhile, working people are often underpaid, brave dangerous conditions, and face the constant threat of unemployment. With or without COVID, the labor market is a cruel game of musical chairs in which hundreds of millions of people search fruitlessly for work while millions more endure precarious employment.

Unemployment is a powerful, if silent, force of economic injustice. It has undermined the foundations of postwar labor relations, the social contract, and workplace solidarity. It looms in every negotiation between unions and firms and opens the door to job outsourcing, race-to-the-bottom pay practices, and the hiring of cheap migrant labor. The threat of unemployment has been and remains the most powerful coercive tool firms wield over their workers. The lives of the unemployed and the employed are thus shadowed by the same fate—the risk of economic insecurity.

The job guarantee[1] proposal aims to end this toxic dynamic by

---

1. Pavlina R. Tcherneva, *The Case for a Job Guarantee* (Cambridge, UK: Polity, 2020).

rising to the call of the Universal Declaration of Human Rights and securing the right to decent work for all people—and to the dignity it brings. The job guarantee is a centrally funded but locally administered public option for good jobs. It is an employment safety net that creates opportunities for the unemployed in long-neglected areas of public purpose—such as health care, community renewal, and environmental remediation. In the United States, it has been hailed as the single most crucial aspect of the Green New Deal agenda. It is a new labor standard for pay and benefits and an alternative to poverty wages in private-sector jobs. It is a stepping-stone for many job seekers and a powerful anticyclical shock absorber for the economy. The job guarantee offers a new social contract—one in which precarious work, communities in disrepair, and an environment in crisis are no longer acceptable casualties in a market-driven economy.

The job guarantee decommodifies work in several ways. First, it ensures that employment offers—that is, the available paid work opportunities—would not depend exclusively on how financially profitable it is to hire people. This is already true of a significant proportion of jobs: in the public and nonprofit sectors, for example, jobs are created not because they generate financial return but because they serve the larger public interest. This may sound strange in an era when we are all accustomed to capitalism's relentless focus on financial profitability, but this type of work is widespread in the economy already. It includes the kinds of activities that provide for our most basic needs: accessible transportation, safety, monitoring, quality control, clean air and water, essential infrastructure, public education, theaters, libraries, and health care. This list is an illustration of the extent to which the things we do in the economy are about providing care: we transport, protect, clothe, feed, entertain, heal, and educate one another. But the profit motive has proven to be ineffective in providing adequate and decent care services for all, meaning that these critical areas remain understaffed and underfunded despite their being central to all human existence. The job guarantee helps meet humanity's neglected needs by matching them to people who can fulfill them.

Second, the job guarantee offers a critical protection for working people. In the modern world, workers (especially those in low-wage jobs) are often treated more poorly than physical or financial commodities. Governments have no trouble intervening quickly in markets to prop up the value of agricultural commodities, oil, and even financial assets when their price drops, rolling out various price supports, buffer stock schemes, and lending programs without batting an eye. Governments are equally responsible for the unemployed, but working people, in contrast to these commodities, are treated as entirely disposable. They are regularly laid off with meager and temporary unemployment protection. A living-wage job guarantee ought to be the minimum necessary employment safety net and protection that governments are obliged to provide, consistent with the objectives of the Universal Declaration.

Third, the job guarantee establishes an uncompromising labor standard for all jobs in the economy, offering dignified employment at family-sustaining wages to anyone who shows up at an unemployment office looking for work. It strengthens the bargaining power of the most vulnerable workers and provides an exit option to working people who experience wage theft, harassment, and discrimination, to name just a few labor market problems. By establishing a secure living-wage floor, below which no working person should fall, the job guarantee pressures private employers to meet and exceed their minimum wage-benefit package to retain and attract workers.

Fourth, inoculating against the enormous social and economic costs of unemployment is in the public interest. The research is clear: unemployment is costly. People are weaker, sicker, and more vulnerable when they experience unemployment. Their mortality increases, and the impact is felt over the long term. Spouses and children suffer many ill effects too, from greater mental and physical health problems to growth stunting and poorer educational and labor market outcomes. Indeed, from the way unemployment spreads from community to community after a sudden shock of mass layoffs to its impact on individuals and their families, it is clear that unemployment behaves like an epidemic—quiet, pernicious, deadly. Governments are then left to deal with the fallout. In the name of job creation, they roll out tax cuts, incentives, subsidies, income support programs of one kind or another, training and education, firm contracts, and loan guarantees—none of which actually create enough jobs for all who need them.

The job guarantee is the most straightforward path to a post-pandemic recovery and tackling the climate crisis—but it must be a permanent policy. Market economies have a rhythm, growing in expansions and shrinking in recessions, and the collateral damage is always people, who are laid off when sales and profitability drop. Thus, the job guarantee is not just another jobs program; it is a structural macroeconomic policy, a countercyclical employment program that expands with recessions (as unemployed people take up public-service work) and shrinks in expansions (as they transition back to the private sector when employment opportunities recover and become more abundant).

Unemployment is a policy choice. In the universe of economic outcomes, there are only two options—guaranteed unemployment or guaranteed employment—and either way, the public sector foots the bill. While unemployment brings large real and financial costs along with negative productivity, the job guarantee inoculates against these costs and directs public funding toward creating socially useful output and superior economic stability.

Making It Happen

Many countries around the world have a network of unemployment offices, often called *job centers*. They provide a range of services to the unemployed, from training and credentialing to résumé building and interviewing skills. The one thing they do *not* provide is any guarantee of actually finding work. Suppose that each and every one of these job centers were converted into a community jobs bank that would solicit and collect project proposals from municipalities, community groups, and nonreligious, nonpolitical, nonprofit organizations. These projects would employ the unemployed in small infrastructure, environmental, and care projects. Like all public options and safety nets, the job guarantee would be federally funded (though in the Eurozone, it would require a Euro-wide funding mechanism). If it were locally administered using a bottom-up participatory design that prioritized the creation and management of projects from the ground up, it would strengthen civil society and local democracy while serving the interests of people and the community.

There are many ways to implement a job guarantee. From the 1930s New Deal programs in the United States to the Swedish tripartite model in which the government effectively acted as an employer of last resort, there is no shortage of useful templates. In the Global South, we can look to programs such as Argentina's large-scale public employment program Plan Jefes; the successful Expanded Public Works Program in South Africa; or to India's MNREGA, currently the world's only legally enforceable right to employment. Although MNREGA is not a universal program (it only provides up to one hundred days of work to a rural household), it has been a crucial lifeline during COVID as the only means of supplying jobs to the unemployed in rural areas.

There are myriad successful youth employment programs too, such as the Youth Guarantee in Brussels, the Future Jobs Fund in the UK, and the Youth Incentive Entitlement Pilot Projects in the United States. In France, the experimental projects known as Zero Long-Term Unemployment Zones (*Territoires zéro chômeur de longue durée*), provide a framework that could be scaled up for the implementation of such a guarantee. Work Integration Social Enterprises can also serve as a useful model for transitioning workers from the job guarantee to private-sector work. What has been missing in this tapestry of programs is the explicit and unequivocal guarantee that whoever is in need of work at a decent living wage can be assured such an opportunity. This moment of historically unprecedented levels of unemployment calls for a new global Marshall Plan for the unemployed, one that creates living-wage jobs, strengthens the public-service sector, and institutes a bold program to remediate the environment.

To decommodify work is not to abolish wage labor altogether, but rather to transform the way in which it is offered. As we *democratize work*, real change would grant working people a say in the rules of their employment. As we *decommodify work*, real change would guarantee economic security for all—including the right to decent employment. As we *remediate the environment*, real change would boost our power and our ability to protect our communities and natural resources. The green job guarantee is a crucial and long-overdue step forward on the path to protecting people and the planet.

*"Without labor investors, there would be no production,
no services, no businesses at all."*

ALL WORKERS PRODUCE VALUE

NEERA CHANDHOKE

Attempts to restore economic growth post COVID-19 will doubt-
less involve economic restructuring, as Pavlina Tcherneva points
out. If current approaches continue, this restructuring will result
in layoffs, increased poverty, and ill-being. It is likely that advanced economies will end up facing humanitarian crises similar
to those experienced in the Global South, which have magnified
the wretchedness of "migrant and informal economy workers," an
unorganized section of the workforce that goes unrepresented in
decision-making structures in factories and firms. I would like to focus here on the importance of expanding voice and decision-making
powers—citizenship, in other words—to this portion of the world's
workforce.

Unorganized labor cannot participate in decision-making and
collective bargaining if trade unions and worker organizations fail
to represent its interests, which is currently the case. The scale of
this problem is alarming: in the Global South, informal workers
comprise an overwhelming proportion of the workforce. In Europe,
large numbers of immigrant workers constitute the dark underbelly
of the formal working class. In the United States, larger numbers of
undocumented immigrants, particularly women, work in miserable

conditions for a pittance. Despite their numbers, their plight and their needs have been largely ignored by unions and other institutions representing the interests of labor. As a result, worldwide, the migrant/informal working class is completely disempowered. We can easily trace a link between the formation of a cheap and unrepresented labor force in the Global South and the creation of wealth in Europe and the United States. Millions of unorganized workers contribute to the production of value-laden goods and services in intricate chains of global production and work, through which manufacturing companies in Europe and the United States subcontract often high-risk and low-paid work to the informal sector in countries in Asia, Africa, and South America. All of these unorganized workers lack basic rights of citizenship. Why is this not of more concern to Western trade unions who determinedly protect formal workers? The main challenge we face in the coming years is finding a way to support the struggle for citizenship rights of formally employed workers while continuing to advocate for better conditions for informal workers.

One reason for the existence of this challenge is the relationship between organized and unorganized workers, which is complicated and contradictory. The two groups complement each other in the production of commodities and services, to which they both add value. Politically, however, they are at odds with each other because unorganized workers tend to undercut the economic interests of the organized working class, which in turn threatens the interests of the entire working class. Given these circumstances, how can we think of work, value, and representation/participation?

The Manifesto gives us an idea of what the answer should be, asking us to recognize that workers are not one type of stakeholder among many: they hold the key to their employer's success. Currently, capital owners monopolize the citizenship rights of firms and other workplaces. It is time to acknowledge that workers are owed rights of citizenship. The logic of the Manifesto's proposition is simple, as Hélène Landemore points out at the beginning of this book: because labor produces value, all workers deserve to have voice in processes that govern the production, distribution, and consumption of that value.

This proposition is particularly important for migrant and unorganized workers, whose lack of citizenship rights has put them at risk. The example of India shows us why universal approaches that include all types of workers, rather than targeted ones, are so crucial. The onset of liberalization in 1991 dissolved conventional distinctions between the formal and the informal workforces. Within the formal organized sector of the economy, increasing use of contract labor with no job security has considerably weakened the bargaining capacity of trade unions. Currently, the organized working class forms a mere 8 percent of the workforce. This is part of what the *Report of the National Commission on Enterprises in the Unorganised Sector*, established by the Indian Government, has referred to as India's "lopsided transformation":[1] structurally, India has not moved from an agrarian economy to an urban-industrial system based on a standard labor contract, worker mobilization, and welfarism.[2]

India's rural sector has been periodically wracked by agrarian distress, and agriculture provides income only to a minority of households. As Pavlina Tcherneva mentioned, the Mahatma Gandhi National Rural Employment Guarantee Act (2005) provides one hundred days of employment per year to one adult member of a poor rural household. The act does not grant a generic right to regular employment. Consequently a majority of rural villagers work as casual laborers outside their villages in the agrarian sector or in cities, jobs that Jan Breman has suggested engender relations of neobondage. Workers incur debt to secure rural and urban employment. Indebtedness creates ready targets for processes of coercion and servitude.[3] The Mahatma Gandhi National Rural Employment Guarantee Act has been unable to alleviate severe agrarian distress. This highlights the urgent need to institutionalize a universal and comprehensive job guarantee program, one capable of tackling both rural and urban unemployment. If democratic governments are serious about their obligations to ameliorate urban and rural poverty, then programs such as the Mahatma Gandhi National Rural

1. Government of India, *Report of the National Commission for Enterprises in the Unorganised Sector* (New Delhi: National Commission for Enterprises in the Unorganised Sector, 2009).

2. See John Harriss, "The Implications of 'Stunted Structural Transformation' for Rural India," *Canadian Journal of Development Studies* 42, no. 4 (2021): 580–589.

3. Jan Breman, *Capitalism, Inequality and Labour in India* (Cambridge: Cambridge University Press, 2019), 183.

Employment Guarantee Act must be upscaled from targeted policies to universal entitlements.

Large-scale, often circular migration practically guarantees low wages and insecure working conditions across the board. In India, as suggested above, unorganized labor constitutes more than 90 percent of the economy. In cities, migrants from rural areas carve out small spaces for themselves in shantytowns earmarked by filthy open drains, overflowing garbage, and ramshackle shelters made of cardboard and roofed with asbestos. They procure employment in the hazardous and exploitative sweatshops of the informal economy, churning out all sorts of commodities, from nuts and bolts to exotic designer clothes. And yet these laborers are simply not considered politically relevant: their voices are unrepresented in the economic and political domain, unattended to by policy makers, and ignored by trade unions.

From 2004 to 2014, representatives of civil society associated with India's governing coalition, led by the Congress Party, recommended a series of social laws to benefit the poor. Civil society organizations moved to support these laws: they spoke the vocabulary of social rights, held public hearings, organized rallies, sit-ins, and processions, and lobbied the media and members of Parliament and State Assemblies. Five campaigns for the right to food, work, education, information, and land bore fruit in the form of progressive social policy, facilitated by a proactive judiciary.

Under the present government, led by the religious and right-wing Bharatiya Janata Party, these social rights have been wiped out and replaced by far weaker policy. Civil society has been pulverized. Many of us believed that once civil and political rights had been secured by the constitution and bolstered by movements for civil liberties, the government and civil society could turn to the work of social and economic rights. We have been proven terribly wrong: under the current government, civil rights, particularly the right to freedom of speech and the right to association, have been suppressed. We have learned two lessons from this experience: first, that rights do not come in stages but rather form an indivisible package; and second, that whereas a democratic state needs civil society, the precondition of civil society is a democratic state.

Without civil society to speak up for them, workers in the informal sector and the poor have become even more vulnerable. On March 24, 2020, a lockdown was declared in India. Unfeeling owners of small- and medium-size enterprises shut their doors on workers; coldhearted landlords demanded rent from penniless tenants; food ran short. Callously, the government stood by and watched as thirty million workers began to walk the long road home toward their villages, their feet torn and bloodied, their backs bent under the weight of their meager belongings, their eyes dimmed by loss of hope, their bellies distended by hunger, and their throats hoarse for lack of water. Most of them had no money at all, nothing but the hope that they would not remain hungry once they reached home. Any expectation that employers would offer succor in times of crisis evaporated. The villages awaiting these thousands of workers are no idyllic Ruritania. With no citizenship rights at home or in the workplace, where can millions of migrant workers turn for help? Who speaks for them?

Contemporary informal labor is everything Marx wrote of the *Lumpenproletariat*: today's informal workers compete with one another for jobs; they are willing to work for long hours in return for what Marx called a "mess of pottage";[4] even as they slog for a pittance they undercut and drive down wages; they are prepared to offer employers an alternative to the organized working class, however exploitative this alternative might be. Of course, all of this destabilizes the bargaining power of trade unions, giving rise to all-too-human feelings of animus from organized workers who feel these pressures bearing down on their own lives. Yet informal workers matter in the same way that formally employed workers do: first because both groups provide value to goods, but above all, because they are all human and possess all the rights and dignities that come with that humanity.

To better define work, should we not shift the focus from categorizing workers as formal or informal and instead identify them by their relationship to the production of value? It is time for us to realize that the formal and the informal sectors of the economy are not separate entities. The informal sector subsidizes the formal economy; it is a necessary precondition for the formal economy. In both economies, workers produce value; in both economies, workers are human. We must recognize the value of their labor wherever they work. This is why I chose this sentence from the Manifesto: "*Without labor investors, there would be no production, no services, no businesses at all.*"

4. Karl Marx, *Capital: A Critique of Political Economy*, Volume I, Book 1 (London: Swan Sonnenschein, Lowery, & Co., 1887), 181.

THE SUBALTERN *WORKER-BODY* SPEAKS; WILL THE PRIVILEGED LISTEN?[1]

FLÁVIA MÁXIMO

Although the thought reflected in the opening sentence of this manifesto is nothing new, it still holds great power, amplifying a message that has resonated among us since the creation of the International Labour Organization (ILO): workers are not commodities. A worker's body is not just another pound of flesh bought and sold in the market. A worker's body is made of spirit, affection, anguish, hope—and *voice*. But are we really listening?

Paradoxically, the world seems to be willing to listen to these *worker-bodies* now that they are muffled by protective masks. It might not be that paradoxical, however: historically, inaudible voices only become intelligible as something like human utterances when they begin to be perceived in the context of life's collective precariousness.

Building on Neera Chandhoke's reflections about the case of India and its informal workers, which *worker-bodies* are we talking about? Or rather, which *worker-bodies* are we *speaking for*? The ILO Report

1. Gayatri Chakravorty Spivak, "Can the Subaltern Speak?" in *Marxism and the Interpretation of Culture*, ed. Cary Nelson and Lawrence Grossberg (Urbana, IL: University of Illinois Press, 1988), 271–313.

on World Employment and Social Perspectives for 2020[2] informs us that 61 percent of the world's workers are informal. As we discuss democratizing workplaces, let us remember that more than two billion *worker-bodies* perform activities that are not protected by formal employment relationships at all.[3] Income inequality between workers from the Global South and North has increased over the past decades,[4] and data shows that the number of bodies working and living in inhumane conditions is expected to rise yet again in 2021.[5]

It is easy to tune into this year's symphony of precariousness and believe that all of it is equally loud, but the truth is that much of it remains unheard. The commodification of life does not ring out at the same volume for all *worker-bodies*, and, as Lisa Herzog points out in her discussion of epistemic injustice, it is brutal to have to repeat this message without being heard. The current pandemic adds new sounds to this symphony: another note of death and suffering, yet more dissonance in the modern/colonial narrative. The sounds we are hearing must be reorganized into new music: we must try once more to redefine the legal status of life at work and the status of the *worker-body* in labor law. Because all bodies are not the same.

Labor, along with everything that accompanies it, resonates throughout our bodies. Yet the discourse of legal subordination tells us that there is no corporeal subjection in labor law. It teaches us that legal control is exerted over the human labor force, not the human body itself. Labor law discourse, by identifying subordination as the core of labor contract, breaks with abstract contractual egalitarianism, which claims that all contracts are entered into by equal parties. Labor law resonates in Eurocentric modernity as a legal revolution, making this asymmetry in human liberty audible and requiring that it be compensated through the legal construction of the employment relationship. Its goal is to ensure that bodies who work are materially free: giving voice to these working bodies as humans, so that *worker-bodies* can speak, even if it is in the ambiguous tones of free/subordinate labor.

2. ILO, *World Employment and Social Outlook*, Trends 2020 (Geneva: International Labor Office, 2020).

3. ILO, *World Employment and Social Outlook*.

4. ILO, *World Employment and Social Outlook*.

5. ILO, *World Employment and Social Outlook*.

But how free are these bodies? Is it *actually* possible to separate labor force from a worker's body? This protective *cantus* allows us to shut our ears to the ways in which labor law, under the veneer of legal subordination as proclaimed by capitalist modernity/coloniality, is built on the subjection of bodies. Labor law's success in protecting the autonomy of the will has been only partial at best: it has created a legal relationship that has aided the expansion of capitalism without guaranteeing sufficient freedom to dispute, discuss, or alter the nature of the contract. From a critical point of view, the employment relationship has created a paradoxical situation in which simultaneously free and subordinated labor relationships keep *worker-bodies* subject to capitalism. This observation is not meant to silence the huge achievements of the modern employment relationship: they deserve to be amplified—but without messianism. And with critique: when we criticize labor law, pointing out the legal coloniality of the employment relationship, we are also defending it[6] because the brutal ongoing destruction of protected employment, however flawed the employment relationship may currently be, is nothing more than a further deepening of racism, sexism, and LGBT-phobia.[7] These are the bodies that are silenced first.

But I would like to remind readers that we must push beyond critique: we must listen. The concrete subjection of bodies made possible by the coloniality of labor law must be denounced: legal subordination makes it possible for labor law to pretend that freedom for *worker-bodies* in capitalism exists—or at least to pretend that it exists equally. It obscures how this concrete subjection in modernity/coloniality is more violent for some *worker-bodies* than for others. Because not all bodies are the same.

Latin American labor law has reproduced Eurocentric storytelling, with its supposedly linear historical sequence of slavery, servitude, and free labor, which exalts the employment relationship as the greatest achievement of freedom in private relations. However, in Latin America's colonization, forms of work did not emerge in a tidy historical sequence that culminated in freedom: servitude,

---

6. See the structural subordination theory created by Brazilian Labor Courts.

7. Pedro Nicoli and Flávia Máximo, "Os segredos epistêmicos do Direito do Trabalho," *Revista Brasileira de Políticas Públicas*, Brasília, 10, no. 2 (2020): 520–544.

slavery, and free labor existed concurrently in its world system,[8] associated with the idea of race, linked to skin color and to gender,[9] a geopolitical identity forced by the colonizer on the colonized to make inferior functions in the social division of labor appear natural—to sell the flesh of dominated people. The hierarchy of the human voice and nonhuman noise is injected into these *worker-bodies*. Because those bodies are not the same.

Indigenous peoples were confined to servitude; Black people were enslaved; European white women were imprisoned in reproductive work; Black and Indigenous women were enslaved domestically, sexually objectified, raped, and exploited; Black women were subjugated as slaves in rural areas and mines. Only white European men could perform free work. This means that in the colonization of Latin America, there was an exclusive association of male whiteness with free work, with wages, with the standard of human—with *voice*. And it persists.

So we must listen. Listen out for the dissonant notes of *legal coloniality* in labor law. We, from the Global South, reproduce modern-Eurocentric legal labor theory in which the human at work is constituted from an anti-Black, anti-Indigenous, and antifeminine foundation imposed by the colonizer. This universalist legal construction of freedom, represented by the employment relationship, presents itself through a fictitious neutrality that equalizes inequalities. And even today, this Eurocentric speech created by and for the white male *worker-body* determines who the epistemic subject in labor law is. This legal discourse is suffocating, and it legitimizes the sexual-racial division of labor in the world and in Latin America.

You must listen. The reproduction of this Eurocentric discourse of legal subordination, without the proper decolonial translation, means that there is a radical fracture between labor theory and its place of applicability in the Global South: the most oppressed subjects in labor relations are, and always have been, the least protected by labor law because free/subordinate labor was and continues to be a legal construction intended for a single type of *worker-body*: the only one considered human; the only one who deserves the illusion

8. Aníbal Quijano, *Colonialidad del poder, eurocentrismo y América Latina* (Buenos Aires: CLACSO, 2000).

9. Lélia Gonzalez, "A categoria político-cultural de amefricanidade," *Revista Tempo Brasileiro* 92, no. 93 (January-June 1988): 69–82.

of the autonomy of will conveyed by legal subordination; the only one whose voice is heard.

This is why mere legal absorption into subordinate work is insufficient to bring about true detachment from the condition of subalternity. It is a complex issue, involving the pluralization of the epistemological foundations of labor law, in particular with regard to who is considered human under labor law and whose voice is heard. It is about the geopolitics and body politics of knowledge.[10] It is about silent ontological labor. This cannot be reduced to the binary modern discourse of formal/informal legal work and to the exclusive search for protected employment. An example of this is the Law 150/15 in Brazil, which recognizes all employment relationship rights for domestic workers. It was an immense achievement, fought for and won by domestic workers themselves, who are silenced in the union legal system. But even with their employment relationships recognized, discrimination persists against such bodies, considered nonhuman. Despite this, and because of this, the loftiest aim of the majority of workers in the Global South, especially those of color, is still merely to attain legal subordination as a privileged place of subjection in capitalism. For such subaltern subjects, the cheapest bodies according to all legal parameters, even the prospect of legal subordination is still a far-off whisper. They remain subaltern flesh, nonhuman flesh, and their voice is diminished to animal noise.

The task of making coloniality in labor law audible is not an easy one, but the radical project of decoloniality in knowledge requires amplification beyond a theoretical whisper. The voice of decoloniality in labor law, and the review of its epistemic subject that entails, must be projected loudly, loud enough to be heard over the sirens of coloniality/modernity. Loud enough to remind us that mercantile time is not the only time that generates value; that those who perform productive work are not the only ones entitled to a minimum income;[11] that the eco-systemic expansion of the concept of the work environment[12] is necessary; that techniques of data gathering and

---

10. Gloria Anzaldúa, *Borderlands/La Frontera: The New Mestiza* (San Francisco: Aunt Lute Books, 1987).

11. See the experience of *Bolsa Família* in Brazil.

12. ILO Convention, no. 190; ILO Recommendation, no. 198.

of biosurveillance at work must be critically reappropriated;[13] that collective bargaining must be redefined;[14] that the time has come for feminist intersectional strikes.[15] Because we can no longer mimic the binary discourse of modernity/coloniality. We are a polyphony of hybrid *worker-bodies*: with colors, with gender, with voices—voices that are definitely not all the same.

In pandemic times, my body, your body—which are not the same—sing many tunes of struggle. It is necessary to claim control over our own bodies. Over our own voices. And there is nothing more powerful in resistance than a *worker-body*. Especially the subaltern one. Who always had a voice, who always knew how to speak, who screams out, who dies trying to be heard: Will the privileged listen?

13. See the Brazilian app delivery strike "#brequedosapps" associated with the app users' boycott that occurred on July 1, 2020.
14. Regarding civil bargaining: Renan Kalil, "As possibilidades jurídicas de organização e atuação coletiva dos trabalhadores informais," *Revista Direito Mackenzie* 7, no. 1 (2014): 188–210.
15. "Ni una menos" in Argentina; "Un violador en tu camino" in Chile.

"Democratize firms; decommodify work; stop treating human beings as resources so that we can focus together on sustaining life on this planet."

SUSTAINING LIFE ON THIS PLANET

ALYSSA BATTISTONI

Sustaining life on this planet in the face of accelerating ecological crises, from climate change to biodiversity loss, while also ensuring good lives and livelihoods for people around the world and reversing the growth of inequality, is the great challenge of twenty-first century politics. Yet too often these are treated as two separate problems: an ecological challenge and an economic one. Perhaps you have wondered while reading this manifesto: How do democratizing and decommodifying work contribute to the remediation of the environment? Conversely, does remediating the environment really require that we democratize and decommodify work? Perhaps you have even worried that democratizing work might make it *harder* to address the climate crisis and other ecological challenges we face. After all, labor and environmental movements have often been at odds over the fate of industries that cause environmental damage but also provide jobs.

Democratizing and decommodifying work are not silver bullet solutions to environmental remediation. But they are a crucial piece of the project of remaking our economies and undertaking the "rapid and far-reaching transitions" that scientific bodies like the

Intergovernmental Panel on Climate Change now say are necessary to avert climate catastrophe.[1]

Democratizing

There are real tensions between environmental and labor movements: many ecologically destructive industries are also the sources of work on which many people depend to make a living. But these tensions are often exaggerated, while a more serious one—between the incentives of firms and the condition of the biosphere—is overlooked. In fact, environmental protections do not come at the expense of labor protections—rather, they often accompany them. Where the power of corporations is unchecked, they are likely to treat both workers and the earth poorly. Yet, workers in environmentally harmful industries have been used as a fig leaf for the executives and shareholders who hold the real power and make the real decisions. Their priority is not good jobs or a healthy planet—it is the bottom line.

As Isabelle Ferreras notes, workers put their bodies, health, and even lives on the line when they go to work each day, and they should have the decision-making power to validate or veto that investment. While workers typically lack that power, it should not be surprising that unions have often been a forceful voice for environmental protections, recognizing that the harmful effects of production are often most concentrated within the workplace. In the 1960s, unionized coal miners in Appalachia demanded improvements to health, safety, and environmental conditions, drawing attention to the crisis of black lung disease in particular.[2] The United Farm Workers raised the alarm about the effects of pesticides on workers' health at the same time that Rachel Carson's *Silent Spring* drew attention to their ecological effects.[3] Tony Mazzocchi of the Oil, Chemical and Atomic

1. IPCC, "Summary for Policymakers," in Global Warming of 1.5°C: An IPCC Special Report on the impacts of global warming of 1.5°C above pre-industrial levels and related global greenhouse gas emission pathways, in the context of strengthening the global response to the threat of climate change, sustainable development, and efforts to eradicate poverty. V. Masson-Delmotte et al. (Geneva, Switzerland: World Meteorological Organization, 2018).

2. Trish Kahle, "Rank and File Environmentalism," *Jacobin* June 11, 2014. Accessed September 2021, https://www.jacobinmag.com/2014/06/rank-and-file-environmentalism/.

3. Chad Montrie, *The Myth of Silent Spring: Rethinking the Origins of American Environmentalism* (Berkeley: University of California Press, 2018).

Workers International Union (OCAW) organized workers exposed to asbestos, eventually helping to pass the Occupational Safety and Health Act (OSHA).[4]

Pollution, waste, and other environmental harms generated in the course of production affect people outside the workplace too, of course—in the United States, those affected are disproportionately communities of color.[5] Shareholders and CEOs are not part of those communities. But workers are, and unions can be a voice for them. As the coal miner and union organizer Jock Yablonski asked in West Virginia in 1969, "What good is a union that reduces coal dust in the mines only to have miners and their families breathe pollutants in the air, drink pollutants in the water, and eat contaminated commodities?"[6] The union, Yablonski argued, should address workers' concerns not only within the workplace itself, but within their broader communities. The Bargaining for the Common Good organizing framework, as pioneered by the Chicago Teachers Union in the last decade, reflects this attitude: unions bargain around the needs of the community at large as well as on traditional "bread-and-butter" issues. It shows how unions can play a role in demanding environmental justice beyond the workplace, working with the communities of which they are a part.[7]

Today, of course, many of the most pressing economic and environmental issues we face extend far beyond the workplace or the community to the level of the planet. The globalization of production has enabled companies to evade democratic accountability by moving social and environmental harm around the Earth. This is no less true of the emerging "green economy": the supply chains of the green energy transition, for example, stretch around the globe, from

4. Erik Loomis, *Out of Sight: The Long and Disturbing History of Corporations Outsourcing Catastrophe* (New York: New Press, 2015): 57; Les Leopold, *The Man Who Hated Work and Loved Labor* (White River Junction, VT: Chelsea Green Publishing, 2007).

5. Laura Pulido, "Geographies of Race and Ethnicity II: Environmental Racism and Racial Capitalism," *Progress in Human Geography* 41, no. 4 (2016): 524–533.

6. Cited in Kahle, "Rank and File Environmentalism."

7. Todd E. Vachon et al. "Bargaining for Climate Justice," *The Forge*, March 31, 2020. Accessed September 2021, https://forgeorganizing.org/article/bargaining-climate-justice; see also "Bargaining for the Common Good: Organizing in the Coronavirus Era and Beyond," *The Forge* Special Issue. Accessed September 2021, https://smlr.rutgers.edu/research-faculty/center-innovation-worker-organization-ciwo/bargaining-common-good/forge-special; on the related phenomenon of "whole worker organizing," see also Jane McAlevey, *No Shortcuts: Organizing for Power in the New Gilded Age* (Oxford: Oxford University Press, 2016).

lithium mining in Chile to battery production in China to electric vehicle manufacturing in the United States.[8] The race to the bottom will slow only when people around the world have the power to challenge companies that seek to extract resources or dump toxic waste as cheaply as possible while using the cheapest labor they can find. Democratizing work across global supply chains could connect workers and communities in different countries in service of improving both labor and environmental standards: at each stage, workers and communities must be involved in decision-making about the labor and environmental standards of production.[9] As Ferreras notes, workers should have the ability to veto or validate the investment of their labor wherever they are in the world.

While democratizing individual firms and production processes is essential, to remediate the environment it is also crucial to democratize the economy more broadly. Policies like sectoral bargaining and codetermination are key to improving the conditions of work across the board and setting standards for industry-wide problems like pollution and toxic waste exposure. Democratizing the economy also means bringing private investment decisions under greater public scrutiny and control. Firms often suggest they are working on environmental problems internally, touting their sustainability programs and decarbonization targets. In recent years, meanwhile, "ethical investment" strategies have become popular, often referred to under the banner of ESG—short for *environmental, social, governance*. But the standards for ESG investing are murky, making it susceptible to greenwashing. Meanwhile, companies' actual commitments to decarbonization and shifts in capital allocation have lagged behind their lofty statements of ambition.[10] We should not, in short, expect companies simply to adopt environmental

8. Thea Riofrancos, "What Green Costs," *Logic* no. 9, December 7, 2019. Accessed September 2021, https://logicmag.io/nature/what-green-costs/.

9. Kate Aronoff, Alyssa Battistoni, Daniel Aldana Cohen, and Thea Riofrancos, *A Planet to Win: Why We Need a Green New Deal* (New York: Verso, 2019); Benjamin McKean, *Disorienting Neoliberalism: Global Justice and the Outer Limit of Freedom* (Oxford: Oxford University Press, 2020).

10. Adrienne Buller, "Doing Well by Doing Good? Examining the Rise of Environmental, Social, Governance (ESG) Investing," *Common Wealth*, December 2020. Accessed September 2021, https://www.common-wealth.co.uk/reports/doing-well -by-doing-good-examining-the-rise-of-environmental-social-governance-esg-invest ing; Simon Jessop and Elizabeth Howcroft, "World's Top Emitters a Long Way from Aligning with Climate Goals," *Reuters*, March 22, 2021. Accessed September 2021, https://

remediation policies of their own accord: the pressures of profitability and competition all point in the opposite direction. Instead, investment writ large must become more democratic through mechanisms like public finance institutions, more rigorous regulation of "green finance" informed by public consultation, and restrictions on institutional investment in environmentally destructive assets.[11]

Nor do green investment standards typically say anything about labor. As capital pours into green investment opportunities, it is particularly important to attend to working conditions within sectors like renewable energy and green tech. Jobs in the renewable energy sector, for example, do not always pay as well as jobs in the fossil fuel industry, but that is not inherent to the work.[12] Coal mining, for example, was always hard, dangerous, dirty work. But after coal miners unionized—after some of the bloodiest union struggles in US history—it was also work that came with a decent wage, health care, and a pension.[13] Unionizing green jobs is an important step toward making them good jobs and toward ensuring that a greener economy is also a more democratic one.

Decommodifying

Not all of the work necessary for environmental remediation and maintenance is work that is currently done in the private sector, and much of it is work that is unlikely to be. Rather than letting the private sector alone determine which kinds of work are worth doing, a program for environmental remediation must assert a strong public role in creating jobs that improve human life and environmental health, regardless of whether they also generate profits. Public-sector work is not fully decommodified, of course: it is still waged work. But it does represent work whose necessity and worth has been decided by democratic publics rather than private companies.

---

www.reuters.com/article/us-climate-change-investors/worlds-top-emitters-a-long-way-from-aligning-with-climate-goals-idUSKBN2BE1HY.

11. Buller, "Doing Well by Doing Good?"

12. Kate Aronoff, "Green Jobs Can Be Just as Good as Fossil Fuel Jobs," *New Republic*, July 21, 2020. Accessed September 2021, https://newrepublic.com/article/158575/green-jobs-can-just-good-fossil-fuel-jobs.

13. Thomas G. Andrews, *Killing for Coal: America's Deadliest Labor War* (Cambridge, MA: Harvard University Press, 2008).

The job guarantee is a key policy for freeing workers from dependence on the labor market, as Pavlina Tcherneva observes. The element of the *guarantee* is particularly important as a source of stability amid the social transformations required to address the multiple ecological crises we face. The job guarantee also gives workers the ability to leave dangerous or environmentally destructive jobs, weakening the power of "job blackmail," which makes workers wary of environmental struggles. Decommodifying access to other essential services, like health care and retirement benefits, that are often linked to work can also give workers greater freedom to organize within their workplaces and to leave jobs that are harmful to their health and environment. The more workers are forced to access the necessities of life through work, the more dependent they are on their jobs and more defensive they are against anything that threatens them, heightening tensions between labor and environmental movements.[14]

The public sector also has a crucial role to play in a just transition: the idea, developed by the labor movement, that workers' livelihoods should be protected even as socially and environmentally harmful industries are shut down. OCAW, for example, proposed a renewed GI Bill for atomic workers left unemployed by nuclear disarmament and a Superfund program designated for worker support. Mineworkers for Democracy called for miners who lost jobs to environmental regulation to be given union work restoring local land or building necessary infrastructure. Today, states can facilitate the urgent transition away from fossil fuels by committing to the likes of wage replacement, health-care coverage, childcare access, and pension contributions for affected workers.[15]

Public works programs are also part of the project of democratizing investment: determining where social funds, resources, and labor are most usefully applied on the basis of social and environmental well-being rather than private profitability. As states set standards for renewable energy production and invest in the infrastructure necessary for decarbonization, for example, they can institute col-

14. J. Mijin Cha et al., *Workers and Communities in Transition: Report of the Just Transition Listening Project* (Labor Network for Sustainability, 2021); J. Mijin Cha, "A Just Transition: Why Transitioning Workers into a New Clean Energy Economy Should Be at the Center of Climate Change Policies," *Fordham Environmental Law Review* 29, no. 2 (2017): 196–220.

15. Cha et al., *Workers and Communities in Transition*.

lectively bargained labor agreements that set wage rates and benefits standards for green infrastructure and technology projects. In turn, setting high standards for work in renewable energy and other environmentally oriented projects can help win union support for further green policies.[16]

Other "green jobs" should be treated as permanent public services rather than fluctuating in relation to economic conditions, as a jobs guarantee program is designed to do, or temporarily ramping up via infrastructure investment, as with public works spending. As Dominique Méda argues, we must care for the earth and other species on it as well as for each other. Care work is itself a kind of green job: it constitutes work that improves people's lives in low-carbon ways.[17] But care workers are often poorly paid and overworked, even as access to care is prohibitively expensive for many people. And care work, both waged and unwaged, is disproportionately done by women, as Imge Kaya-Sabanci observes, contributing to gender inequality. Care should be treated as a public good: made accessible to all and with high standards for wages and working conditions.[18] The work of caring for the earth, meanwhile, is for the most part not acknowledged or paid at all. During the Great Depression, however, the Civilian Conservation Corps was a hugely successful but temporary source of public employment, undertaking everything from flood control to soil conservation to wildlife aid. Today, a revived CCC committed to the crucial work of ecological restoration and maintenance should be made permanent, while Indigenous land stewardship should be recognized and rewarded.[19]

16. Betony Jones, Peter Philips, and Carol Zabin, *The Link Between Good Jobs and a Low Carbon Future: Evidence from California's Renewables Portfolio Standard, 2002–2015* (Berkeley: Center for Labor Research and Education, University of California, 2016).

17. Alyssa Battistoni, "Living, Not Just Surviving," *Jacobin*, August 15, 2017. Accessed September 2021, https://jacobinmag.com/2017/08/living-not-just-surviving/.

18. Gabriel Winant, *The Next Shift: The Fall of Industry and the Rise of Health Care in Rust Belt America* (Cambridge, MA: Harvard University Press, 2021).

19. Neil Maher, *Nature's New Deal: The Civilian Conservation Corps and the Roots of the American Environmental Movement* (Oxford: Oxford University Press, 2008); *The Red Nation, The Red Deal: Indigenous Action to Save Our Earth* (New York: Common Notions, 2021); Nick Estes, "Indigenous People Are Already Working 'Green Jobs'—But They're Unrecognized and Unpaid," *Intercept*, September 23, 2019. Accessed September 2021, https://theintercept.com/2019/09/23/indigenous-climate-green-new-deal/.

Many of these expansions of public-sector work can and should be paired with the decommodification of the goods and services necessary to live a good and ecologically sustainable life. Decommodifying and expanding public transit can give workers an alternative to long commutes in private vehicles, helping to remake resource-intensive transportation patterns while creating permanent transit jobs. Expanding social housing in dense, transit-served areas can contribute to lower-carbon models of living, ease the pressure on workers struggling to keep up with skyrocketing rents, and create both construction and long-term maintenance work.[20]

Moving toward an ecologically sustainable society does not only mean creating new kinds of work, however—it also means working less. Shorter working hours, long a demand of the labor movement, give workers more time to spend as they will, while also reducing carbon emissions.[21] Decommodifying public space by creating parks, libraries, and museums that are open to all can make it possible for people to enjoy their free time in low-carbon ways: enjoying the company of other people, the outdoors, art and music, and the other pleasures of life.[22]

A good life is not necessarily a resource- or carbon-intensive one, and good work does not have to destroy the conditions of life on Earth. But these changes cannot be made at the level of the individual: they have to be made at the level of society as a whole. Democratizing and decommodifying work may not solve our ecological crises on their own. But they are crucial to remaking our economies and societies in ecologically sustainable ways.

20. Daniel Aldana Cohen, "A Green New Deal for Housing," *Jacobin*, February 8, 2019. Accessed September 2021, https://jacobinmag.com/2019/02/green-new-deal-housing-ocasio-cortez-climate.

21. Juliet Shor, *Plenitude: The New Economics of True Wealth* (New York: Penguin Press, 2010).

22. Kate Soper, *Post-Growth Living: For an Alternative Hedonism* (New York: Verso, 2020).

WORKING AGAINST AN END

Shifting Gears for a New Beginning

DOMINIQUE MÉDA

As the author of another widely read manifesto once observed, capitalist production develops only "by sapping the original sources of all wealth—the soil, and the laborer."[1] That is the central lesson of our times: the crisis this era has produced is a crisis for nature—and for workers too. The COVID-19 pandemic was a warning shot, an expedient reminder of the immense vulnerability and great fragility of our societies. We must learn all we can from it if we are to survive. The crisis of the pandemic left our capacity for production intact: energy, telecommunications, agriculture, infrastructure—all were untouched. The catastrophes caused by climate change—hurricanes, floods, droughts, fires—will not do the same. Human activity provoked the disastrous circumstances in which we find ourselves today, which include the possibility of the earth's temperature rising by 6 or 7°C before the end of the century[2]—global warming far more intense than even the most pessimistic forecasts had previously predicted.

---

1. Karl Marx, *Capital*, translated by Samuel Moore and Edward Aveling (Hertfordshire: Wordsworth Editions Limited, 2013), ch. 15, section 10.

2. According to recent estimates by French scientists working in the Climeri-France climate modeling center, who have contributed two models to CMIP6, a global climate modeling initiative, one developed by the CNRM in collaboration with CERFACS, and

Put baldly, it would mean an end to human life on Earth. "Authentically human life on Earth"[3] will vanish—unless we heed the warning and shift into gear for a new beginning.

Our Responsibility: To Grapple with the Past—
To Assure Our Future

Who is responsible? Is it humanity as a whole, driven by greed and a lust for power? Those who say so have dubbed our era the Anthropocene. Others prefer to call it the Capitalocene or the Occidentalocene, noting the far greater fault in a few specific countries that unrelentingly promoted a model for productivity that focuses obsessively on exponential profit growth. Whatever name we choose, the major goal of questioning our past is to help define our responsibility to the future: whether or not each member of the generations currently living on this earth actively participated in the processes that are now forcing us to radically change our lives, we all must actively participate in slowing these processes down—and even stopping them entirely. Together, we must find the momentum necessary to embark—as individuals and as societies—on what I have called an ecological upshift.[4] I use this term as a way to call attention to the need for a radical and very concrete shift in our behaviors and mentalities. As we have discussed throughout this book, the path ahead demands that we not only agitate for change but innovate and orchestrate ways to provide widespread support to our planet and our societies as we traverse a period that will likely resemble—on an even greater scale—the massive industrial restructuring many countries have experienced in the past.

Revisiting Metrics:
Ecological Upshift Begins with a Radical Paradigm Shift

As the American ecologist Aldo Leopold was already suggesting in the 1940s,[5] an ecological upshift would begin with renouncing

one in collaboration with the IPSL. More than twenty climate modeling centers around the world are involved in CMIP6 and together have designed some thirty different models.

3. Hans Jonas, *The Imperative of Responsibility: In Search of an Ethics for the Technological Age* (Chicago: University of Chicago Press, 1984).

4. Dominique Méda, *La Mystique de la croissance. Comment s'en libérer* (Paris: Flammarion, 2013).

5. Aldo Leopold, *A Sand County Almanac* (Oxford: Oxford University Press, 2001).

the relationship of conquest and exploitation human beings have maintained with nature for so long and replacing it with a relationship of respect, admiration, and even love. To embark on an ecological upshift is to exchange exploitation for the imperative to *care*—not just for nature but for all the species that constitute it, including human beings. From there, we must go on to shift our perceptions, our cosmology, and our disciplines to fit this new paradigm.

One example suffices to show the necessity of such a major shift in our frames of reference: since the close of World War II, we have all been obsessed with *growth*—with GDP growth, that is. The conventional aggregate of gross domestic product is a construction of the now ubiquitous System of National Accounts, whose handbook is maintained by the world's five largest international institutions.[6] This indicator and its limitations caused great outcry in the 1970s and again in the 1990s.[7] GDP does not account for much of the activity that keeps society functional, including domestic labor, volunteer labor, or civic activities. This means that it is also unable to take note when they come under threat. The commodification and monetization of domestic labor, for example, might leave families exhausted or threaten the safety of our children and our elders—but it drives up GDP. Nor is GDP affected by inequalities in consumption or production. If 10 percent of a population overconsumes while the rest struggles along with little or nothing, if 10 percent of the working-age population participates in creating market output while the rest are unemployed or underemployed, GDP will not take note of it. Furthermore, national accounting systems based on GDP consider *all* production useful, even when it is highly toxic. But above all, GDP does not include any assessment of two crucial forms of wealth: nature and social well-being. Working conditions may be hellish, or they may help workers flourish; inequality may be vast, or it may be minimal; our air may be pure, or it may choke us at every breath—but no matter. While these limitations have been highlighted before,

6. The World Bank, the European Commision, the International Monetary Fund, the Organization for Economic Cooperation and Development, and the United Nations.

7. See Dominique Méda, *Au-delà du PIB. Pour une autre mesure de la richesse* (Paris: Champs-Flammarion, 2008); Méda, *La Mystique de la croissance*; Florence Jany-Catrice and Dominique Méda, *Faut-il attendre la croissance?* (Paris: La Documentation française, 2016); Isabelle Cassiers, Kevin Maréchal, and Dominique Méda, eds., *Post-Growth Economics and Society: Exploring the Paths of a Social and Ecological Transition* (London and New York: Routledge, 2017).

notably by the Commission on the Measurement of Economic Performance and Social Progress in 2009, no alternative indicator has been put in place. The havoc it wreaks is old news now—Donella Meadows et al. described it in great detail nearly half a century ago in *The Limits to Growth*—but for want of anything better, we continue to worship at the altar of GDP. It is urgently necessary to enact strict social and environmental limits on GDP—on the growth process, in other words. New wealth indicators, in particular carbon footprints and the index of social health, must be adopted.[8]

Shaping the Inevitable:
Ecological Upshift as Proactive Crisis Prevention

If we truly wish to decarbonize our economies and achieve carbon neutrality by 2050, as ratified in the Paris Agreement—and as survival on this planet requires—business operations in many sectors will have to shut down, while many others will have to greatly overhaul their manufacturing processes. At the same time, many new businesses will need to be launched and developed. This massive change will require massive labor mobility, and organizing it should not be left to chance. We have seen what happens when it is: the huge restructuring of Europe's textile and steel industries, the intensification of global trade, offshoring and other tremendous changes that came with it, the reorganization of value chains, new international divisions of labor—all of these have occurred in ways that left those most affected by them by the wayside. At best, they are shunted into early retirement or unemployment; in all too many cases, they are left without any source of revenue at all.

An ecological upshift means proactive anticipation; it means meeting these changes head-on. This is not only to protect the people affected by them but also because such massive transformations in the labor force would no doubt mobilize populations in protest. Ecological upshift is impossible without the kind of "just transition" that unions, in particular the International Trade Union Confederation,

8. For years, along with my colleagues Florence-Jany-Catrice and Jean Gadrey, I have been calling for these new indicators to be adopted. See Dominique Méda, "Promouvoir de nouveaux indicateurs de richesse: histoire d'une 'cause' inaboutie," FMSH-WP-2020–142, June 2020.

have been demanding for several years now. The coming transition will not count as an upshift if it happens in a way that harms those in the unlucky position of working in jobs that will disappear because they are, for one reason or another, too harmful to the environment.

Ending the Race to the Bottom:
Ecological Upshift Must Raise Us All

The ecological transition *must* happen now. As it gathers momentum, we should do everything in our power to ensure that the process is organized in ways that anticipate which sectors will shut down or be restructured to the point that their labor force must find new work. We must map the skill sets employed in these sectors, along with the competencies required for the new jobs created in new sectors that will open up and expand, to ensure people in need of jobs are matched with the work that will need to be done. This will necessitate a high degree of precision and large-scale public policy tools so that labor can rapidly transition from shrinking sectors into expanding ones. Restructuring must happen at every level: internationally, nationally, and locally.

As many studies have revealed, an ecological upshift would create many jobs.[9] This does not mean that smooth conditions for labor mobility will occur out of nowhere—nor does it imply that the market will take care of them. It is imperative for us to create effective support mechanisms. A crucial one of these is the job guarantee Pavlina Tcherneva (p. 85) describes in her contribution, which would provide a stable revenue and employment status for people exiting sectors that are shrunk or shut down or whose professions change dramatically as this inevitable transformation occurs. A job guarantee is therefore an indispensable tool for effective environmental upshift and should be implemented alongside policy measures for effective training and social support programs, perhaps in partnership with initiatives such as the One Million Climate Jobs Campaign,

---

9. ILO, *Emploi et questions sociales dans le monde 2018: Une économie verte créatrice d'emploi* (Geneva: Bureau international du Travail, 2018); Guillermo Montt et al., "L'action pour le climat, une action contre l'emploi? Évaluation des conséquences du scénario à 2° C sur l'emploi," *Revue Internationale du travail* 157 (2018): 573–613.

which is calling for the creation of public climate agencies that would be put in charge of hiring and training people whose jobs will disappear in the climate upshift. This would facilitate rapid reemployment in sectors that will experience growth, such as retrofitting buildings, repair and recycling, infrastructure, the greening of manufacturing processes, etc.

Democratizing:
An Ecological Upshift Depends on Giving Voice to All

In all cases and for all organizations affected—both in sectors that must undergo massive restructuring to stop their greenhouse gas emissions, cease polluting, and quit decimating biodiversity as well as in sectors that will grow—another key to the success of the ecological upshift will be the democratization of companies and of the economy in general. When they read the Manifesto, some of the people who signed it—or chose not to—pointed out that company employees might not be ideally placed to organize the disappearance of their own jobs, and they remarked that it was necessary to include our natural environment as one of the constituents of all human organizations.

Certainly, we have seen employees fighting to keep their jobs when their companies shut down—think, for example, of workers in the nuclear sector protesting plant closures—and we have seen that their protests garnered union support. Is it not only fair for workers to try to protect their jobs and to fight to keep exercising their professional skills? What choice have they had but protest? We must acknowledge that the democratization of companies to which we aspire, and which must take place, might not necessarily lead employees to take positions favorable to the environmental upshift, particularly in cases where the upshift would require their companies to close. That is why the Manifesto's second proposal must go hand in hand with the first if we are to hope for the success of the third: anticipatory measures such as the job guarantee would make it possible to decommodify work, thereby bolstering the democratization of firms in a way that would change the stakes entirely for decisions made with—or even by—workers. If workers, along with their union representatives, could have a voice in the government of their companies—that is, in setting the strategies of their organizations, in the precise mapping of their skill sets and desired jobs, in the organization and management of local monitoring agencies and branches, and in the design of new productive organizations to take the place of the firms required to close or restructure—it is to be expected that employees in companies affected by the ecological upshift would become actively involved in all of these. In this context, all of the energy being poured into fighting decisions companies make in the sole interests of their capital investors could be channeled into the creation of new organizations to support the ecological upshift.

Giving voice to our natural environment and to future generations is crucial for a successful upshift, which raises the practical question of who might best represent them. Environmental organizations are an obvious choice, but the criteria for selecting the right organizations for the job must be set democratically. Another option would be consumers: their voice is also an essential one, and they might build coalitions with labor and nature representatives under any number of circumstances. Although the place of these constituents in the decision-making process is important, we must be careful to avoid muffling the collective voice of companies' more central constituents—their workers. If we do not, we risk drowning out worker voices in revamped forms of corporate social responsibility, an approach that, as we have seen all too clearly over the past thirty years, has been pitifully ineffective at protecting both workers and our planet. Never has CSR made it possible for an organization to escape the extractive worldview that dominates capital interests when they are left to themselves.

It is urgently necessary to accede to workers' demands to participate fully in the decision-making processes of their organizations and to expand that right to all workers. Such a change would bolster the resilience of our societies, which is vital if we wish to heed the warning shot of today's crisis. It is clear that the climate crisis will bring challenges whose scale and contours we probably cannot even imagine. As the Manifesto makes clear, rising to those challenges requires that we focus on three inextricably linked principles: *democratize*, *decommodify*, *remediate*. Together, they will guide us as we shift to the task of rebuilding our societies on new foundations, offering a roadmap away from the paradigm of conquest and exploitation with a simple key: *to care*—for one another, for our future, for our planet.

▶

ACKNOWLEDGMENTS

The publication of this manifesto on May 16, 2020, happened through the gracious volunteer efforts of researchers and citizens who came together from around the world in the space of two short weeks. We wish to thank the following people for their work in coordination, support, communication, web design, and more: Brittany Butler, Julien Charles, Devin Clark-Memler, Lukas Clark-Memler, Olivier Jégou, Colleen Kelly, Médiatrice Nkurunziza, Alicia Pastor y Camarasa, Ally Philip, Barbara de Radiguès, Kara Sheppard-Jones, Anna Skarpelis, Joseph Vaessen, Gaëtan Vanloqueren, and Mu-Chieh Yun.

For translation and media contacts in their respective countries, we would like to thank the following: Christine Abbt (Universität Graz), Melanie Adrian (Carleton University), Rodrigo Arocena (Universidad de la República, Uruguay), Jonghoon Bae (Seoul National University), Armi Beatriz Bayot (University of Oxford), Eyja Margrét Brynjarsdóttir (University of Iceland), Laurence Castillo (University of Melbourne), Gianfranco Casuso (Pontificia Universidad Católica del Perú), Laura Centemeri (CNRS–Centre d'étude des mouvements sociaux EHESS), Neera Chandhoke (University of Delhi), Nizzan Zvi Cohen, Alex P. Dela Cruz (University of Melbourne), Filip Dorssemont (UCLouvain), Susanne Ekman (Roskilde University), Pablo Fernández (IAE Business School/Universidad Austral), Valentina Franca (University of Ljubljana), Maha Ben Gadha, Luiz Gustavo da Cunha de Souza (Universidade Federal de Santa Catarina), Olli Herranen (Tampere University), Adolfo Rodríguez Herrera (Universidad de Costa Rica), Agasef Imran (Economic Think), Florence Jany-Catrice (University of Lille), Fadhel Kaboub (Denison University), Imge Kaya-Sabanci (IE Business School), Daniel Kotecký, Hannes Kuch (Goethe University Frankfurt), Arto Laitinen (Tampere University), Auriane Lamine (UCLouvain), Xavier Landes (Stockholm School of Economics in Riga), Sari Madi (University of

Montreal), Mubariz Mammadli (UNEC), Massimo Maoret (IESE
Business School), Isabelle Martin (University of Montreal), Flávia
Máximo (Universidade Federal de Ouro Preto), Roberto Merrill
(University of Minho), Adam Mrozowicki (University of Wrocław),
Natavan Namazova (UNEC), Paulo Savaget Nascimento (Durham
University and University of Oxford), Olga Nowaczyk (University
of Wrocław), Serena Olsaretti (ICREA–Universitat Pompeu Fabra),
Mikołaj Pawlak (University of Warsaw), Dick Pels (University of
Amsterdam), Israr Qureshi (Australian National University), Periša
Ražnatović, Ingrid Robeyns (Utrecht University), Halil Sabanci
(IESE Business School), Sebastián Pérez Sepúlveda (IRISSO, Uni-
versité Paris Dauphine-PSL/UCLouvain), Miguel Simón-Moya,
Virginia Simón-Moya (University of Valencia), Riccardo Spotorno
(Universitat Pompeu Fabra), Foad Torshizi (Rhode Island School
of Design), Mitsuhiro Urano (Kwansei Gakuin University), Frederic
Vandenberghe (Universidade Federal do Rio de Janeiro), Cecilia
Varendh-Mansson (University of Oxford), Marc Ventresca (Uni-
versity of Oxford), Scott Viallet-Thévenin (Université Mohammed
VI Polytechnique), Nicholas Vrousalis (Erasmus University Rotter-
dam), Sophie Weerts (Université de Lausanne), Clare Wright (La
Trobe University), Toru Yoshida (Hokkaido University), Lea Ypi
(London School of Economics), Justo Serrano Zamora (University
of Groningen), Zivar Zeynalova (Anadolu University).

We are deeply grateful to Miranda Richmond Mouillot, who
translated the chapters originally written in French for *Le Manifeste
Travail*, published by Le Seuil in Paris in the fall of 2020. She also
edited the chapters adapted or written exclusively for the English
edition and worked closely with all the authors to make sure this was
a whole new book offered to an English-speaking audience.

We warmly thank Chad Zimmerman, our editor at the University
of Chicago Press, whose support of and belief in this group endeavor
were an irreplaceable source of encouragement. We could not have
wished for a better partner. The whole team at the University of
Chicago Press has been stellar.

We are truly grateful for the many invitations we have received
since May 2020 to discuss the Democratizing Work Manifesto and
its three principles, the results of which are only partially reflected
in these chapters. In particular, we are very grateful to Josh Cohen
and Marshall Ganz, who were invaluable to us in the last stretch

of the writing process. We would also like to extend our heartfelt thanks to Sandra from Vida Verde for sharing her story with us and to Isabella De Toni for helping translate it. We are very grateful to Nan Stone for her precious feedback and suggestions. As for producing the book, we are profoundly thankful to our wonderful research team: Leszek Krol, Julie Krzanowski, Libby Quinn, Kara Sheppard-Jones, and Alexandra Ubalijoro at Harvard and Camille Guenane at the Royal Academy of Belgium. Without them, we could not have published this book. We would also like to thank the Social Innovation and Change Initiative team at the Harvard Kennedy School.

Finally, the thirteen female scholars who wrote this book did so as a contribution to the movement that they, as the core group of organizers, are building with the network of signatories of the Democratizing Work Manifesto. As with the other translated adaptations of this book, all royalties from sales will be donated by the authors and will go toward sustaining the ongoing efforts of the #DemocratizingWork movement.

We thank everyone who has engaged in this conversation for the past two years, from within academia and beyond. We look forward to discussing this book with all its readers as we work toward an economy that meets our democratic commitment to the equal dignity of workers and to the remediation of the environment.

Join the global conversation. Sign the Manifesto!
Get involved via www.DemocratizingWork.org.

ABOUT THE AUTHORS

JULIE BATTILANA is the Joseph C. Wilson Professor of Business Administration at Harvard Business School and the Alan L. Gleitsman Professor of Social Innovation at Harvard Kennedy School, where she is also the founder and faculty chair of the Social Innovation and Change Initiative. In addition to numerous articles in scholarly journals and the press, she is the author of *Power, for All* (New York: Simon & Schuster, 2021) with Tiziana Casciaro.

ISABELLE FERRERAS is a senior tenured fellow (*maître de recherches*) at the Belgian National Fund for Scientific Research in Brussels (*FNRS-Fonds de la recherche scientifique*), a professor of sociology at the University of Louvain (IACCHOS_CriDIS), and a Senior Research Associate of the Labor and Worklife Program at Harvard Law School. She is an elected member of the Royal Academy of Sciences, Humanities, and the Arts of Belgium, Class Technology and Society. Her publications include *Gouverner le capitalisme? Pour le bicamérisme économique* (Paris: Presses universitaires de France, 2012) and *Firms as Political Entities: Saving Democracy through Economic Bicameralism* (Cambridge: Cambridge University Press, 2017).

HÉLÈNE LANDEMORE is a tenured associate professor of political science at Yale University. Her publications include *Democratic Reason: Politics, Collective Intelligence, and the Rule of the Many* (Princeton, NJ: Princeton University Press, 2012) and *Open Democracy: Reinventing Popular Rule for the 21st Century* (Princeton, NJ: Princeton University Press, 2020).

LISA HERZOG is an associate professor at the Faculty of Philosophy and the Center for Philosophy, Politics and Economics of the University of Groningen. Her publications include *Reclaiming the System:*

Moral Responsibility, Divided Labor, and the Role of Organisations in Society (Oxford: Oxford University Press, 2018) and *Die Rettung der Arbeit* (Berlin: Hanser Berlin, 2019).

IMGE KAYA-SABANCI is a management scholar, with a focus on entrepreneurship and strategy, at IE Business School in Madrid. Having worked in international organizations, the private sector, NGOs, and universities for more than a decade, she has extensive experience in a range of international development programs focused on entrepreneurship, women's economic empowerment, and gender equality.

ADELLE BLACKETT is a Professor of Law and the Canada Research Chair in Transnational Labour Law and Development at the Faculty of Law, McGill University. She is an elected fellow of the Royal Society of Canada. Her numerous publications include the award-winning book, *Everyday Transgressions: Domestic Workers Transnational Challenge to International Labor Law* (Ithaca, NY: Cornell University Press, 2019) and the special guest edited issue, "Transnational Futures of International Labour Law," of the trilingual *International Labour Review* Vol. 159, no. 4 (2020).

SARA LAFUENTE is a researcher at the European Trade Union Institute (ETUI receives funding from the European Union) and the Université Libre de Bruxelles. Some of her recent publications are "The Road to Pan-European Codetermination Rights: A Course that Never Did Run Smooth," in Johannes M. Kiess and Martin Seeliger, eds., *Trade Unions and European Integration: A Question of Optimism and Pessimism?* (London: Routledge, 2019), 158–177, and "Negotiated board-level employee representation in European Companies: Leverage for the Institutional Power of Labour?" *European Journal of Industrial Relations* Vol. 25, no. 3 (2019): 275–289.

JULIA CAGÉ is an assistant professor of economics, Sciences Po-Paris, a codirector of the Laboratory for Interdisciplinary Evaluation of Public Policies in Paris, and a research associate at the London Center for Economic and Policy Research. Her publications include *Saving the Media: Capitalism, Crowdfunding and Democracy* (Cambridge, MA: Harvard University Press, 2016) [*Sauver les médias. Capitalisme, financement participatif et démocratie*] (Paris: Le Seuil, 2015).

PAVLINA R. TCHERNEVA is an associate professor of economics and Director of the Economic Democracy Initiative at Bard College. In addition to numerous scientific articles on modern monetary theory and unemployment and employment policy, she is the author of *The Case for a Job Guarantee* (Cambridge, UK: Polity Press, 2020).

NEERA CHANDHOKE is a professor emerita of political science at the University of Delhi and the former director of its Developing Countries Research Centre. Currently, she is a Distinguished Fellow of the Centre for Equity Studies in New Delhi. Her many publications include *Rethinking Pluralism, Secularism, Tolerance: Anxieties of Co-Existence* (Delhi: Sage, 2019), *Democracy and Revolutionary Politics* (London: Bloomsbury Academic, 2015), and *State and Civil Society: Explorations in Political Theory* (Delhi: Sage, 1995).

FLÁVIA MÁXIMO is an associate professor of labor law and social security law at the Universidade Federal Ouro Preto, Minas Gerais, Brazil. She is the author of "Decolonial Thinking and Brazilian Labor Law: Contemporary Intersectional Subjections," *Revista Direito e Práxis, Rio de Janeiro* 9, no. 4 (2018): 2117–2142, with Daniela Muradas, and *Labor Law and Dissident Epistemologies*, Elgar Studies in Labor Law (Cheltenham: Elgar, forthcoming in 2022) with Pedro Augusto Gravatá Nicoli.

ALYSSA BATTISTONI is an assistant professor of political science at Barnard College in New York City. She is the coauthor, with Kate Aronoff, Daniel Aldana Cohen, and Thea Riofrancos, of *A Planet to Win: Why We Need a Green New Deal* (New York: Verso, 2019).

DOMINIQUE MÉDA is a professor of sociology and the director of the IRISSO (Institute for Interdisciplinary Research in the Social Sciences) of the Université Paris Dauphine-PSL, where she holds the Ecology, Work, and Employment chair of the Global Studies program of the FMSH. Her numerous publications include *Post-Growth Economics and Society* (New York: Routledge, 2019), with Isabelle Cassiers and Kevin Maréchal, eds. and *Reinventing Work in Europe: Value, Generations and Labour* (Cham, Switzerland: Palgrave Macmillan, 2017) with Patricia Vendramin.

INDEX